Halftime Adjustments

The Gen X Guide to Dominating Our Second Half

Brian J. Moore

New Linxus Publishing, LLC

DEDICATION

This book is dedicated to the memory of my mother, Sarah J. Moore. They say you learn everything you need to know in kindergarten. I learned everything I needed to know on the morning of my first day of kindergarten. Undoubtedly sensing her son's nervousness, my mother said "just do your best – that's all you can do!" This book is premised on the simplest advice being the best. Thanks Mom!

CONTENTS

INTRODUCTION

Don't look now, but Generation X is middle-aged. There are about 50 million of us, born between the early 1960s and early 1980s. You are holding in your hands the ultimate playbook for our generation's "second half." We were called the slacker generation, lazy, and disloyal. We shattered those myths and have already accomplished a lot. Unfortunately, we're also facing hard times. The reality of the world we live in has changed. Many of us are not living the lives we set out to lead, or accomplishing the things we wanted to achieve. We've also seen what happened to the baby boomers, a generation who thought they had it made, only to be trapped in the harsh reality that many of them will never be able to retire.

As a fellow Gen X member, is your life going exactly the way you wanted? Personally, career-wise, and financially? Great! You're well ahead of the curve - and probably the type of person who will enjoy reading through this book for refresher training and some new tips to help you continue dominating life. As for the rest of us, *Halftime Adjustments* will help us make the necessary changes in order to rebound and enjoy a successful second half. Let's be clear. This is a book for overachievers who have overachieved at certain aspects of their lives, while ignoring or not giving proper weight to other areas. If you have achieved some degree of success, but still feel like you are not where you need to be, this is the book for you. This is not a book for underachievers, unless you are truly ready to change your ways. If you are, *Halftime Adjustments* will help you take control of your mind, develop a positive attitude, and begin to immediately and dramatically improve your life.

The good news is that our generation is only at halftime. We still have time to make the necessary adjustments to dominate our second half in all respects: setting and achieving goals, time management, leadership, work-life balance, relationships, and personal finance. If you are a boomer or millennial, feel free to come along for the ride. This book contains useful principles that anyone can apply to immediately improve their personal and professional lives. Whoever you are, it's time to leave behind your fear of failure, exit your comfort zone, and start building your dream life. In a funk? Not motivated? Learn how taking the smallest action will create all the motivation you need to take more action. The more action you take, the better you will become at all aspects of life. And the more motivation you will have to continue. If you are willing to read this book, then stand up and take action, you will become a master of achievement, time management, and life in general. You will also learn how to better balance your work and personal lives, strengthen your leadership skills and relationships, and get your financial house in order. While developing yourself in these areas, you will also discover how to effectively use your mind as a tool to better control your life, instead of letting your mind control you.

1 GENERATION X AT HALFTIME

Time is the wisest counselor of all.

- Pericles

What is a Halftime Adjustment?

We know what halftime adjustments are in sports. Whether a team is winning or losing, there are always adjustments they need to make in order to ensure a successful second half of the game. This book isn't about sports though – it's about our lives. When I'm not writing or speaking about personal development and leadership, I'm a lawyer. I work in labor and employment law, helping organizations and people with various issues that arise in the workplace. Recently, I was speaking with a client who we'll call Tim. He's an "in-house" corporate lawyer, and a member of Generation X, like me. When I first met him, I asked about his legal career, expecting to hear that he had started as a judge's clerk or with a law firm, and then eventually transitioned into a corporate position. I was surprised to learn that his legal career had started just a couple of years earlier. Prior to that, he had worked a blue-collar job in manufacturing. He always had an itch to study the law. He finally scratched that itch – at a time in his life when many of us would say it is simply too late. It took sacrifice. Studying for and taking the Law School Admissions Test ("LSAT") and completing three years of law school meant that Tim did not have a lot of time for lazing in front of the television and other so-called "fun" activities. He completed his legal education while balancing an active home life including a wife and children. Tim had made an important decision. He had created a burning desire in himself to become a lawyer and he would stop at nothing to achieve that goal. He did what most people describe as "impossible" or "too hard" – he made a halftime adjustment.

That's what this book is all about. Like it or not, our generation is middle-aged. If we keep doing the things we've always done, we generally know what to expect during the second half: more of the same. We will likely become moderately more successful, make moderately more money, and get in moderately *worse* physical shape. If we want more than that out of life, we need to make some adjustments, and we need to make them now. Maybe the adjustments you need to make don't include a major career change like Tim's, but unless your life has gone perfectly so far, there are probably areas in which you would like to improve. This book will help get you where you need to be in all areas: goal-setting, motivation, time management, career, work-life balance, health and wellness, leadership, relationships, and personal finance.

Who am I to tell you how to live your life? I'm a Gen X'er, just like you: a regular guy who has had his share of ups and downs. Sometimes I've flown high. Sometimes, quite frankly, I've spent too much time "down in the dumps," sleepwalking through life, or paralyzed by procrastination and indecision. I've made some really smart decisions, and some really dumb ones. Along the way, I've managed to achieve a fair amount of success. After growing up quite poor financially, I went to college and then law school. I worked my way up through the law firm ranks to become a partner in my early 30s. I am married to a wonderful woman and have a couple of great kids. I am not really wanting for anything.

Throughout my adult life, however, I noticed there was something gnawing away inside me. I felt as though I was not quite achieving at the level I knew was possible – in several areas of life, including time management, achieving goals, relationships, wellness, and personal finance. I would fall into ruts where I would get up, go to work, come home, eat dinner, and then watch television for a couple of hours before passing out asleep. I felt like there was something missing. I believed it was possible for me to play at a "higher level," so to speak. Like many of my friends (and probably you), there were lots of things I was going to do "someday." I took no real action on any of these things, however, until I began the process of transitioning away from television and other distractions. I became obsessed with books on leadership, personal finance, and personal development. Then, one day, I transitioned into another phase. I stopped reading so much. I started doing. I started speaking and writing to teach others that personal development should be a daily part of our lives. I also tucked myself away in a room one day by myself with no phone, no family, no friends, and no co-workers. Just a laptop and my thoughts. Not a soul on earth other than me knows what I wrote that day. I can tell you it was all about playing at a higher level. If I was going to do that, I knew, at what some people might call "middle-age," I didn't have any more time to waste. That day changed my life. I had made a halftime adjustment.

The book that inspired me the most leading up to that fateful day was published way back in 1932. It's called *Think And Grow Rich* by Napoleon Hill and it's now in the public domain, so you can download and read it for free. I highly encourage you to do so – as soon as you finish this book, of course. Hill's book is not about becoming rich, unless that is what you decide you want to do. It is a book about creating a burning desire for something, and then going for it. My burning desire is to play on that higher level of which I was thinking – to do all those things I had been thinking about doing, including publishing a book that I had been working on for years (not this one). Why hadn't I finished it? I was paralyzed with fear. Fear that people would criticize me. Fear of failure. I decided that playing at a higher level required me to place those fears on the back burner or, even better, to discard them entirely. After all, most of what we worry about never comes to fruition. So, I finished the book. You know what? I survived just fine.

Somewhere along this path I was traveling, it hit me that others in my generation were going through the same exact thing. I wasn't the only one who felt like I wasn't living up to my full potential. Many of my friends were also at or approaching middle-age and realizing that they had to start playing with a sense of urgency if they wanted to squeeze the most out of life. That was the inspiration for this book. It's not a book about me. It's a book about us. Our generation. We are at halftime in our lives. We have been very successful. We can, however, accomplish so much more. We can play at a higher level in all respects, and still have time to relax. Our second half playbook starts with Chapter 2. First, let's take a look at how we arrived at this point.

Generation X

Our generation was born after the post-World War II baby boom, generally between the early 1960s and the early 1980s. Depending on which years are included in the calculation, estimates of the size of Generation X range from 40 to 60 million. We'll use 50 million as a rough estimate. In any event, there are certainly a lot of us, but not nearly as many as there are the baby boomers, the post-World War II children - our parents - of which there are about 80 million. Likewise, there are not nearly as many of us as there are the millennials, those born between about 1984 and 2002. There are almost 80 million of them too! So, Generation X is sometimes called the "sandwich" generation, the "forgotten" generation," or the "niche" generation. Don't let that get you down. As you will see below, we have a lot of qualities that set us apart. We are poised, during the second halves of our lives, to truly dominate.

Major Events That Shaped Our Generation

Like any generation, there have been many major events that shaped us. We remember the gas shortages of the late 1970s. We recall the AIDS epidemic, the Iran-Contra scandal, and the Challenger explosion making headlines in the 1980s. We witnessed White House scandals and controversial military missions filling the headlines in the 1990s and 2000s. In recent years, unfortunately, we experienced a global economic collapse that no one saw coming, and that we will hopefully never have to live through again.

There have been plenty of positive events too. We have witnessed the end of the Cold War and the election of the first black president. The changes we have seen in technology have been nothing short of breathtaking. Many of us remember as small children getting up from the couch to manually change the television channel and maybe even adjusting the antenna for each channel we wanted to watch. We remember the earliest computers and video games, as well as MTV going on the air in 1981. We experienced the birth of 24-hour news and hundreds of new channels available on cable and satellite television. More recently, we've seen the explosion of the internet, smart phones, texting, social media, and other forms of communication and technology that would have been unimaginable to us as children. Even the concept of traditional television viewing is becoming antiquated with so many shows available online for on-demand viewing.

Learning From the Baby Boomers

Those who fail to learn from the past are destined to repeat it. So, let's learn from the baby boomers. It was not too long ago when they were leading lives filled with success – and excess. They had it all. They were financially better off than previous generations, dominated the management structure at work, and really did not know what hard times were like. They enjoyed a runaway stock market in the 1990s, fueled by the so-called "dot com" boom. If you were at all interested in the market during that time period, you know that you could almost throw a dart at a list of stocks and find a winner. Or just invest in any company with a name ending in ".com" – it was that easy and we all thought we were geniuses. Of course, the boomers were the ones in their peak earning years, so they invested heavily – and they made a lot of money – for a while.

They also enjoyed runaway home values. Getting rich was easy. You bought a house, let it rise in value for three or four years, then sold it for a nice profit and moved into a larger one. The combination of the stock and real estate markets left the boomers thinking that they could do no wrong. Surely American society had evolved to the point where everyone could enjoy upper middle-class lifestyles, large homes, fat retirement accounts, and luxury sedans in the driveway.

Some financial analysts issued warnings - what goes up must come down. They asked whether we remembered Black Monday, October 19, 1987, when the Dow Jones Industrial Average fell a whopping 22.61%. They pointed out that the U.S. stock market had historically returned about 9.4% per year, not the 20-30% the boomers were coming to expect. These warnings were dismissed as naysaying by most boomers. They were simply living in a new reality, fueled by the internet and technology. They were smart enough to prevent another Black Monday from happening. Simply put, they had it made! So, boomers stopped accounting for all scenarios. They failed to prepare for the possibility of hard times. They placed their retirement investments in the hot technology stocks of the day. They didn't need to make any halftime adjustments because they were on cruise control.

Then the bubble burst. The "dot com" collapse in 2000 should have served as a warning not to place all of our investment eggs in one basket. The stock market quickly recovered, however, and soared to new heights, this time fueled by a new bubble involving real estate. Just a few years later, the unthinkable happened. Investors had gotten so greedy for more money that risky real estate investing caused major banks to fall on seriously hard times, some even failing. This, of course, set off a domino effect, as the stock market dropped and dropped, then dropped some more, and home values plummeted. The very investments that had made boomers rich were thrusting them into economic turmoil. Homeowners were faced with the reality of owing hundreds of thousands more to the banks than their homes were worth. Retirement account values dropped by half or more. Then, people started to lose their jobs and unemployment skyrocketed. While the stock market has recovered since that time, we are definitely living in a new economic reality. There are simply no sure things in life.

General Characteristics of Our Generation

Early on, commentators described Gen X as materialistic, disloyal, and disenfranchised slackers. As it turns out, Gen X is characterized by highly educated, entrepreneurial, active, motivated, and family-oriented individuals. We value work-life balance, health, and wellness, and we have high rates of volunteerism. Simply put, we are very well-rounded.

While keeping in mind that any description of an entire generation is necessarily a generalization, Gen X members typically distrust authority figures, believe they can only truly rely on themselves (hence the entrepreneurial spirit), and are strong advocates of personal choice. There are good reasons for this. In our lifetimes, we have learned that everyone is human and that we are more likely to find a hero in our own neighborhood than in Washington, D.C. or Hollywood. We have learned that there are no secrets anymore. The mass media and bloggers leave no stone unturned. We have learned that there is no loyalty in the corporate world. We watched as the baby boomers devoted their careers to big secure companies, only to be laid off in return. Simply put, we have learned that we have to rely on ourselves, not our parents or the government. We are the only ones who can bail ourselves out.

Why the Second Half is So Important

We only get one crack at this thing called life and, as a generation, ours is about half over. As in sports, the second half is when we find out whether we won or lost. You can still win the game even if you got off to a slow start or find yourself playing with a huge deficit. But it is going to take time, you need a game plan, and you need to start now. No more procrastination. It's time for action!

Questions to Ponder

1. Think back to your early adulthood. What were your hopes and dreams for life? What did you want to accomplish? Where did you think you would be by this point in your life?

2. Is your life going according to plan? If not, what areas need improvement?

3. If you could change one thing about your life, what would it be?

2 GET MOTIVATED TO TAKE ACTION

A burning desire to be, and to do, is the starting point from which the dreamer must take off. Dreams are not born of indifference, laziness, or lack of ambition.

- Napoleon Hill

Taking Action

This was originally the last chapter of the book, with its goal being to inspire you to go forth and take action. Then it dawned on me that maybe the pep talk should come first – so that you are motivated to finish the book and follow at least some of the advice contained within it – which will undoubtedly require you to take action and work hard. This chapter is all about goal-setting and motivation. Along the way, we will review some of the obstacles we face in these areas, such as fear, indecision, and procrastination.

Setting Goals

Why set goals? So you can accomplish them! It's as simple as that. What do you want to accomplish in the next year? Two years? Five years? What is your overriding goal in life? Is it to become CEO of a major corporation? Is it to win political office, build a successful business, or improve the community in which you live? Is to be the best parent possible? What is the one thing you would like to accomplish but presently believe is impossible?

We all know deep down that it is important to set goals. If you don't, it is highly unlikely that you will achieve your full potential. Results do not randomly occur. We must force them to occur. We love to flirt with thoughts about what we would like to accomplish, but it is rare that we actually devote significant time to turning those thoughts into reality. Ask five of your friends what their goals are for the rest of their lives, for the next five years, or just for the next year. A majority of them will not be able to answer the questions and will likely show signs of discomfort at being asked. Indeed, these are difficult questions to answer. Just thinking about them may be frightening. If you are going to make the most of your remaining life, however, you are going to have to devote significant time to developing your goals. Once you have decided on these goals, you may or may not decide to share them with others. You probably should not share them with everyone. You probably should, however, share them with your closest confidants. This will not only provide you with a great support system, but will help you feel more accountable as you get to work.

Writing Down Your Goals

You have heard this advice before. You absolutely must write down your goals. This step is critical but easy to overlook. You may be thinking, "I'll write down my goals later." Promise yourself that, after you have finished this book, you will take pen to paper, or get out your favorite electronic device, and write out your short and long-term goals. Begin with your goals for this coming year. We all do this anyway with new year's resolutions. Take a more formal approach this time. What do you *really* want to accomplish this year, both personally and professionally? Thinking longer term, what do you want to accomplish over five years? Your lifetime?

When you write out your goals, you will realize things about yourself that you never even considered before. There is something magical about putting words to paper (or a screen) that helps you realize the things in life that are truly important to you, the things you really want to accomplish, and the things you thought were important, perhaps because others led you to believe they were, but really aren't that important to you.

You are never going to fully appreciate what you want to accomplish in the near and long term unless you write out your thoughts and engage in some truly introspective thinking. If you are having trouble with this task, try this: find a place where you can be alone with your thoughts and a writing instrument. No other people, no television, no phone, no music, no internet, no print media, no work, no anything. Brainstorm with yourself and truly think about who you are and what you want to accomplish. Jot down ideas and goals that pop into your head. Spend as much time as you need. When you are finished, you can organize what you have written and consider whether to delete or add items. Once you have finished your initial set of written goals, remember that these do not have to remain set in stone. You can revisit them from time to time, decide if they are still what you really want, and make adjustments as necessary. Your initial goal-setting may take some time, especially as you try to determine your overriding life goal. You may spend a year or more on this phase. Once you have a workable product, however, most of the job will be done, except for occasional review and adjustments.

So far, we have been discussing "big picture" life goals, but you can and should write out your more mundane goals for shorter time periods. Some people like to make a written plan for their week on Sunday evening or Monday morning. Some make written plans daily. Yes, you can probably take it too far, but you get the idea. How are you going to accomplish anything if you don't write it down and visualize what needs to be done?

No matter what time period you are planning, think about the one thing you just *have* to accomplish during that time period. That is your most important goal and should be the centerpiece of your planning.

So, you have written down some goals. Now the real fun begins! Keep reading to learn how to turn your "thoughts" about these goals into the "reality" of achieving them, including how to overcome some of the obstacles you will meet along the way.

Accomplishing Your Goals

The very first step in accomplishing your goals is to *believe* that you can accomplish them. Not just believe a little. Truly believe. The mind may be the most powerful force in the universe. You can accomplish, or fail to accomplish, anything using the power of your mind. Napoleon Hill coined the phrase "thoughts are things," and that is true. If you can think it, you can accomplish it. There is no such thing as an impossible goal. Think back to any important accomplishment in your life. Have you achieved things that other people said weren't possible, or that you initially told yourself you couldn't do? Continue thinking back and appreciate that, at some point, you told yourself that you *could* accomplish each of those achievements. They didn't randomly happen. You willed yourself to accomplish them. Every achievement and every invention began as a thought in someone's head. Pause and think about that. Does that help you appreciate the remarkable power of the human mind? Most of us are walking around using *maybe* 20 percent of our mind's capacity. We are just sleepwalking, or going through the paces, in our personal and professional lives. While 100 percent may not be realistic, imagine if we truly became engaged and increased the percentage to 50 or even 70 percent.

Notwithstanding the title of this book, I have attempted to keep the sports clichés to a minimum. Permit one more. When the game is over, you don't want to have lived your life on the sidelines - you want to have been out on the field, in the midst of the action. You want to have left everything you have on that field. This entire book can be summed up in one word: action. It is what separates success from failure. It is what separates the rich from the poor. It is what separates the fulfilled from the unfulfilled. In order to truly accomplish great things, you must think them, believe in them, prepare your plan, and then put your plan into action. It is that simple. There are, however, some stumbling blocks you may have to overcome along the way.

Indecision and Procrastination

Indecision and procrastination are huge problems. If we are not careful, they can cost us years of following our dreams. Do any of the following thoughts sound familiar?

- "Someday I am going to go back to school."
- "Someday I am going to look for a better job."
- "Someday I am going to get in better shape."
- "Someday I am going to write a book."
- "Someday I'll ask her out."
- "Someday I'll start saving for retirement."

Quite often, "someday" never comes. We have become quite good at thinking about doing things, but not so great at actually beginning the process of doing them. Indeed, the main difference between highly successful people and others is that the highly successful people actually took action to accomplish their goals. Imagine if our Founding Fathers had never gotten past the "someday" phase of wanting to take action. Imagine if Thomas Edison had never gotten past the "someday" phase of inventing the electric light bulb. The solution to indecision is easy. Just take some action, no matter how small. As we'll see in the next section, one small action can lead to very oversized results.

Motivation

If you are like me, the biggest obstacle to taking action is lack of motivation. Motivation does not automatically happen. Something has to happen for you to become motivated. Sometimes you have to hit rock bottom before you are willing to change. Maybe a health problem will help you become serious about diet and exercise. Maybe being laid off will motivate you to find another job. I finalized this book after realizing that I had let it sit for two years, likely due to fear, procrastination, and indecision. These are negative events, however. Waiting for a negative event to motivate you is very *reactive*. Wouldn't you prefer to be *proactive*? There is a positive practice you can develop that will serve to motivate you. Action. There's that word again. If you are suffering from lack of motivation, try taking some action, even if it is a very small one. While this may be uncomfortable at first, taking action will actually help create the motivation you need to take more action. More action will create more motivation. You'll see a snowball effect. Think of a diet or exercise. When you first start, it is awkward, uncomfortable, and easy to quit. Once you have devoted some time to it, you become more motivated and committed. You don't want to lose your investment and, once you learn that you can do it, you become more and more motivated to continue doing it. If you have ever written a book or lengthy publication, you know that it is tough to get motivated to write those first few pages. The more action you take, however, and the more pages you compile, the more motivated you become to finish the project.

After realizing that I had let this book sit for two years untouched, I forced myself to take one tiny action – print it for editing. That one small action started a snowball effect, yet it was the hardest part of finishing the project. This principle applies to any activity in life that you want or need to do. Actually doing it will motivate you to do more. So, instead of waiting to become motivated, take a little action now and the motivation will come naturally.

Exit Your Comfort Zone

Risky truly is the new safe. The only way to really get ahead in life is to take some risks. I'm talking about calculated risks, not reckless ones. Regardless, risk-taking requires you to leave your comfort zone, at least for a little while. What is it that makes us fear leaving this imaginary little place? You know - that zone where we do the same things we have always done in our personal and professional lives - because we know what we can expect when we do those things. We wake up every day and go through the same scripts and routines. We don't rock the boat. We don't try new things because something might go wrong and we might end up embarrassed or worse. This keeps us safe. Unfortunately, it also keeps us from reaching our full potential.

The only way to achieve true success is to venture outside of this safe little zone. How do you do that? Start small. Exit your comfort zone briefly and take action you wouldn't normally take. Prepare first so you have a pretty good chance at success. You'll find that the experience is not nearly as bad as you imagined. Of course, you will be uncomfortable. That's why it's outside of your comfort zone. The more time you spend there, the more comfortable you will get being uncomfortable. That is where you will find your greatest achievements in life. What if you decided to spend a month or even a year outside of your comfort zone, as sort of an experiment? What's the worst that could happen? Well, horrible things might happen to you, just like you feared. There's not much lasting harm to that. You could retreat to your comfort zone for the rest of your life - and you would have the knowledge of knowing what happened when you committed yourself to living outside of that safe place. The more likely scenario, however, is that you will test yourself like you have never been tested, and, as a result, you will begin to accomplish more than you ever dreamed possible. All because you engaged in that initial small action of stepping outside of your comfort zone to see what the world really looked like.

Get Out of Your Head

The mind is a powerful tool. The mind can also consume us with obsessive thought patterns. For example, many people have a tendency to dwell in the past, either on past positive events ("my life was better back then") or past negative events ("I don't deserve happiness because of what I did back then"). Equally as debilitating is obsessively thinking about the future. Again, this can be positive ("my life will be better when *this* happens") or negative ("what am I going to do if *that* happens?"). Many people live their whole lives waiting for something better to happen to make them happy. The problem with all of this obsessive thinking, whether about the past or future, is that it is all fiction. You are not thinking about actual events as they happened in the past. You are thinking about your version, or your story, about what happened. There is no way that story can be accurate because every life event is subject to an infinite number of interpretations. These interpretations become even more skewed over time. As for the future, it has not even happened yet. So, anything you think about it is obviously fiction. The only reality is the present moment. That is always where life is lived. So, get out of your head and start actually living life.

Fear of Failure

The main fear that prevents most people from taking action to improve their lives is the fear of failing. Failure is awful. What if we fail and, even worse, people make fun of us and/or criticize us for attempting to reach our goals? Let's get one thing straight. Failing is not fun and I am not going to try to convince you otherwise. Failure is, however, a necessary part of life. It is a necessary component of growth. It is a necessary ingredient for ultimate success. No matter how conservative and risk averse you are, you are not going to make it through life without failing at many things.

Think of any successful person you know and I guarantee that person has failed many times. Winston Churchill flunked out of sixth grade and lost every election of his career before becoming British Prime Minister at age 62. Colonel Harland Sanders received over 1,000 rejections of his chicken recipe before he founded Kentucky Fried Chicken. Producers told Marilyn Monroe she was not pretty or talented enough to be an actress. Walt Disney was fired from a job for having a lack of imagination. Jerry Seinfeld was booed offstage during his first stand-up routine.

You just don't know about these failures because these people were not famous when they failed. The failures were not newsworthy. We only hear about successes and think that those people are somehow more talented, more gifted, or just plain better than us. Sometimes they are. More often than not, though, the difference is simply that these people were not deterred by failure. Successful people get over their failures, learn from them, and exercise persistence until they accomplish their goals. Thomas

Edison, known as one of the greatest inventors in history, failed many times before achieving his greatest successes.

So, we know failure is an inevitable part of life. The question then becomes why should we fear it so much? Accept it as normal. Get over your fear. It is not the failure that is holding you back. It is the fear. The fear is just a creation of your mind. It is a fiction. The sooner you get over this fear, the easier it will be for you to achieve success. When you fail, you face a fork in the road. You have two choices. Let the failure debilitate you and force you to quit, or keep going, refusing to give up, until you achieve your goal. Choose the second path and let it lead you to a more accomplished and fulfilled life. As for criticism, you are not going to make it through life without being criticized, no matter what you do. So, learn to live with it and don't let it bother you. Author Elbert Hubbard is often credited as saying "to avoid criticism, do nothing, say nothing, and be nothing." Wouldn't you rather be something?

Fear of Success

The fear of failure probably makes sense to you. Who would want to fail? No one. But have you ever stopped to consider whether you suffer from the fear of success? What happens if your hopes and dreams come true? Will your friends and family still like you? Will you be able to handle it? Will you become a different person altogether? Ask yourself these questions and see if you might actually be afraid of success. Other symptoms include thoughts such as "those types of things don't happen to me" or "am I the right type of person for this?" The root cause of this fear is often another fear: the fear of change. We become extremely comfortable with the current state of affairs. Changing ourselves, even for the better, is uncomfortable because it is different. Just like the fear of failure, you will have to work hard – at first – to minimize dwelling on the fear of success. Like most fears, you should be able to acknowledge that the fear of success is essentially irrelevant and a waste of time. It is also a completely fictional creation of your mind. So, if this fear is troubling you, start by ignoring it, just a little at a time. Then, the busier you become actually accomplishing your goals, this fear will start to fade away naturally. When you feel it start to creep back in from time to time, remind yourself of its irrelevance to your life. Over time, you will become good at minimizing your fear of success, and that will prevent it from sabotaging your life.

Positive Versus Negative Thinking

You may think this topic is common sense. Engage in positive thinking and resist negative thinking, right? Like many of the concepts discussed in this book, however, this one is simple to understand, but much more difficult to implement.

We have all experienced friends who may have actually turned out to be the opposite of friends - they were negative influences on our lives. Unfortunately, we all share a mutual and long-term friend who likes to visit us. If you let this friend take up residence in your mind, they will get quite comfortable. So comfortable that you may find their presence reassuring in some perverse way. This friend's name is Negativity. Even after you break off the friendship, they will still try to come around. They may even comfort you. After all, once you give in to them, you no longer have to work as hard. You don't have to devote as much energy to wondering whether you will accomplish your goals - because you know you won't. Deep down though, you know that Negativity is sabotaging your life.

We need to eliminate negative thinking. This will not happen overnight and it is hard work. In order to do this, you have to actively instill positive thoughts into your head. You never have to work on adding negative thoughts. They will enter your mind automatically. Your job is to work towards adding positive thoughts to displace the negative ones. Many books have been written on the power of positive thinking. This one section of one chapter cannot possibly replicate the entirety of those volumes. There are some general tips that will help you, however. First, remember that things are neither good nor bad. We just think they are good or bad. We make the conscious (or subconscious) decision to place labels on events. Second, remember that thoughts are constantly occurring in our heads. We can't stop them for long. We can choose whether to follow a particular thought stream and dwell on it, letting it gain power and take control of us. If there is a negative thought that occupies your mind, you are making the choice to let it rule your mental space and tax your energy levels. You can make the opposite choice. You can choose to let go of that negative thought. You can choose not to dwell on it. Try this: when you feel the negative thought stream beginning, just say "STOP!" to yourself in your head. Then, think about something positive. Maybe this sounds overly-simplistic. It is. We overthink most things in life and overlook the simplest solutions. It really works and you will see an instant improvement in your mood – and probably your blood pressure!

Over time, the best way to minimize negative thoughts from entering our minds is to add more and more positive thoughts, even if we have to force them into our minds at first. This can be as simple as saying to ourselves every morning three things we are looking forward to during the remainder of the day. Then keep adding from there. The more positive thoughts running through your head, the less room there will be for negative ones. Imagine a lawn filled with weeds. How do you get rid of those weeds? You can pull them or spray them – temporary solutions. That is similar to the "STOP!" concept discussed above. If you really want to get rid of the weeds and stop them from coming back, you have to create a lawn so chock full of healthy grass there is no room left for weeds to grow. Applying this concept to our thoughts sounds simple, but it will take a lifetime to master. I have been working on it for years, and will continue working on it the rest of my life. Thankfully, like most things, the more you practice, the easier it becomes to replace your negative thoughts with positive ones.

Persistence

Persistence is not giving up at the first sign of defeat. Those who have accomplished great things have accomplished them through persistence. They simply would not take "no" for an answer. Have you ever worked at a problem and been unable to solve it the first seven, eight, or *fifty* times you attempted it? But you kept at it and wouldn't take no for an answer? Then, lo and behold, there was a successful attempt? You stuck with it until you got it. That is proof positive in the power of persistence. The problem is, we don't stick with most things. We give up too early. Why do we do that? Is it because the goal was not that important?

Is it because of a fear of failure? Is it because of a fear of success? Regardless of the reason, it is clear that if we truly want something and we persistently go after it, we will obtain it.

Continuous Incremental Improvement

Most of us have experience with new year's resolutions. "I'm finally going to get in shape this year by going to the gym five times a week." "I'm going to pay off all my credit card debt." "I'm going to stop eating junk food." Most of us also have experience with failing at these resolutions. One of the main reasons we fail is because we set "all or nothing" conditions and then, when things don't go just right, we think we have failed and we drop the resolution, until next year of course.

What if, instead, we simply said to ourselves "I'm going to exercise just a little more next week than I did this week" -- how difficult is that promise to keep? Not very difficult at all. Instead of improving 100% at once, we just do it a little at a time and then repeat. Eventually we will see a snowball effect and, before we know it, we will have improved many times over. Several books have been written about this concept. If you are interested in reading more, check out Darren Hardy's *The Compound Effect* and Tom Connellan's *The 1% Solution for Work and Life*.

Go Forth and Take Action!

You now have the tools you need to finish this book, implement its advice, and dominate the second half of your life. You don't have to read the chapters in any particular order – this isn't a novel. It is your playbook to help you correct some areas of life where you may have gone astray – or areas you may have ignored completely. As you read each chapter, you may find yourself wanting more in-depth study of a particular topic. Check out the *Recommended Reading* list at the back of the book.

Like anything worth pursuing, you have to continually practice personal development. Keep this book handy and refer to various sections when you feel yourself struggling or losing motivation. Try to do something each morning that will inspire you to action, whether it be reading, writing out your plans, or engaging in some reflection or meditation. Over time, you will develop a personal development "consciousness." The more you do something, like engaging in personal development activities, the more opportunities you will see to engage in further personal development, including helping others do the same. Life can be a long arduous journey, if we let it control us. Hopefully, this book will show you that, if you take control of your life, just about every activity you engage in can be enjoyable, peaceful, and enlightening.

Questions to Ponder

1. What would you like to accomplish one year from today? Three years? Five years?

2. What is your overriding life goal (i.e., the one thing you just *have* to accomplish)?

3. What is one goal you would like to accomplish, but believe is impossible?

4.   What steps are you going to take to begin working towards these goals?

5.   When will you start taking even the smallest action towards accomplishing these goals?

3 WE'VE STILL GOT TIME, BUT . . .

He who every morning plans the transactions of that day and follows that plan carries a thread that will guide him through the labyrinth of the most busy life.

- Victor Hugo

Has the first part of your life gone by quickly? The second part is going to go even faster. Then it will be gone. Don't panic. We've still got a bunch of time left, but we absolutely must adopt the habit of using it wisely. Upon reading the description of this book, you may have thought to yourself, "I know personal development is important, but I just don't have the time!" Indeed, that is a common refrain among our generation (and everyone for that matter). No one has enough time. Generation X has come far enough to realize that time is absolutely *the* most precious commodity we have. Time is opportunity. It is an opportunity to make money, if you want or need to make money. It is an opportunity to relax, if you want or need to relax. It is an opportunity to have quality interactions with your family and friends, and you definitely need to do that.

We all complain that we don't have enough time. Ironically, however, we also can't deny that we waste a lot of it. What should you do with a precious commodity? Throw it away? Of course not. You would never do that with diamonds or gold. Time is much more valuable than either of those things. So why do we waste so much of it? Well, unlike diamonds or gold, we are all given a great big chunk of time (life) absolutely free. We can do whatever we want with it. Combine this with the fact that we do not like to acknowledge the possibility of our own deaths, and we create an illusion that we have an unlimited amount of time – all in the future, of course. We never have enough time *right now* for all the important things that we want or need to do.

The fact is we will all die someday and our time is limited. This should not be a depressing realization, but an enlightening one. Our lives and time are gifts to be appreciated. If we, as Generation X, want to squeeze everything we can out of the second halves of our lives, we need to minimize our wasting of time.

The number one way you can stop wasting time is to become more time conscious. When you are time conscious, you are always analyzing the most efficient and effective use of your time. This chapter will show you how to do that. As you practice and become better at time consciousness, you will find that you begin to do it subconsciously, not even having to think about it. This is not a new concept. Thomas Jefferson was obsessed with the efficient use of time. He kept clocks in every room of his home to remind him to use each minute wisely.

The first step to becoming time conscious is to "mine for time," by taking a look at some areas where we may be wasting time, or where it may be hiding. Then, we will create an easy action plan for making the best use of the additional time we discover, including prioritizing the activities that are most important to us. This process should be fun, not work. So, bring a positive mental attitude with you as you get started. As Eckhart Tolle points out in *The Power of Now*, life is always lived in the present moment. It is never lived in the past or future. So, you always have a choice: enjoy this moment or don't. I promise you will have a much smoother and more peaceful life if you adopt the habit of enjoying each moment. So, with that in mind, let's get a handle on managing our time.

Mining for Time: Electronic Time Wasters

Boom! Right off the bat – you knew I would say it, right? Although we recognize how incredibly valuable time is, we waste a lot of it, especially with technological "time wasters." In our defense, we were the first generation to be completely overwhelmed with such things – and they are pretty amazing. We started out as children with basic television and radio. At or approaching middle-age, we've experienced 500-channel cable and satellite television, video games, computers, cell phones, the internet, smartphones, tablet computers, countless gaming apps on every device we have, and numerous forms of online social media and entertainment options. Wireless internet service is available just about everywhere, even in cars. It has gotten to the point that we are almost offended if we don't have instant access to our email, the internet, and/or our gadgets. These are all incredible tools that can be used in healthy moderation. They can also overtake our lives, leaving us little time to accomplish any meaningful goals. Time is our most precious commodity, yet we often give it away freely to our beloved electronic toys. In fact, the number one way most of us could gain more time is by cutting back in this area.

We fail to realize that, in some ways, these technological tools are oppressing rather than liberating us. We joke about it, like when one popular device was likened to crack cocaine a few years ago. This is a serious matter, however. We can't let technology control us. We have to control it. We don't have to completely cut electronic devices from our lives. As with everything, moderation is the key. See if you can exercise a little self-restraint. Try checking your social media sites once or twice per day instead of every few minutes. Try the same thing with email and texts. Try not taking on any new television programs this year. Try to cut back on the programs you don't truly enjoy but just feel obligated to watch. Try a video game or social media blackout for a few days or even a week. At the end of that time period (after a twitchy first day or two), you are likely to find that you don't miss the technology as much as you thought you would. Instead, what you are likely to end up with is more time on your hands – time to do those important things you have been meaning to do.

Mining for Time: Bedtime

Another big area where you may be wasting time is getting ready for sleep, sleeping, and "waking up" after sleep. Do you go to bed before you are truly sleepy, then flip through the television channels or surf the internet on your electronic device? This could be a valuable piece of time. Try working on a more productive activity (like an important goal) until it is really time for bed, then you can go to sleep without any distractions.

As for sleep time itself, studies have generally shown that the average adult needs seven to eight hours of sleep per night. If you are sleeping more or less than that, there are likely adjustments you need to make in other areas of your life (diet, exercise, caffeine, and health come to mind). The work-life balance chapter will help you with those.

Do you have trouble getting out of bed in the morning? After a full night's sleep, the answer should be "no." Unfortunately, many of us do have trouble getting active in the morning. If this is due to being tired, then you know what adjustments to make. Examine your true feelings though, and see if there is a deeper darker reason why you aren't that excited to jump out of bed each day. Are you afraid of life? I know that sounds funny. Of course, you're not "afraid" of life in the same sense as being afraid of a wild animal. I'm talking about a general unease regarding life. Think about this for a moment. Do you mask your unease by distracting yourself? As you truly think about this, are you afraid of what the day may be bring? Afraid of failing? Afraid of succeeding? All of the above? These may seem like silly suggestions until you really examine your feelings to see if any of these fears are present. As I mentioned earlier, there was a point where I let this book sit mostly finished without taking any action to on it – for two years! Why? I thought about it for awhile and the bottom line was fear. Fear of criticism. Fear of failure. What is the easiest way to deal with these fears? Bury your head in the sand! What does that accomplish? Absolutely nothing, but we all do it in various aspects of life. Why try and fail when we can do nothing and "not fail"? Fear explains a lot in life. It holds us all back. It may be the real underlying reason why, instead of jumping out of bed in the morning, excited for the day, you mindlessly peruse social media sites on your phone or immediately turn on the television to distract your mind. Our subconscious fears may run concurrently with bouts of mild depression, which we all get. The combination can cost us years of valuable time. Resolve with me now not to let this hold us back any longer.

Mining for Time: Incremental Time

We have many untapped sources of time in our lives. The problem is, many of these sources consist of only small increments. It is convenient to ignore and waste these small periods of time. If we add up all these little increments, however, they would amount to one huge chunk of time. If only we could somehow think of creative uses for that time. We'll tackle that later, but let's first take a look at some examples of where we might find this so-called incremental time.

We thought we were busy when we were in school or during our early adult years. As we approached middle-age, however, we realized just how easy we had it back then, and how much free time we actually had. If you have kids, you have countless birthday parties, sporting events, and other appointments on your calendar, which is already full of work activities, community involvement, and household chores. Throw in some social engagements with friends and you can quickly become overwhelmed. None of these events are going away anytime soon.

What we are truly losing, however, is not only the time directly associated with these events, but the time around them as well. We tend to waste a lot of these small increments of time. Let's take a look at an example. On a particular Saturday, you are scheduled to go for a run with your friend from 7:00 to 8:00 a.m., a birthday party at your son's friend's house from 2:00 to 4:00 p.m., and a dinner with friends at 6:30 p.m. The time actually spent in these events is valuable time. You are exercising, spending time with your family, and strengthening your relationships. All great things. If you pay close attention, however, you will likely find that you waste a lot of additional time around these events. You may be up and ready at 6:00 a.m., but the run is not until 7:00 a.m., so what do you do with that small chunk of time? You may have an hour between the end of the birthday party and the time you need to start getting ready for dinner. What do you do with that hour? Do you tend to just sit idly waiting for the event to begin? Get out your phone and mindlessly scroll through social media posts? Maybe flip through the television channels? Well, whatever the case may be, you are wasting valuable incremental time.

Other incremental time can be found in the following places: right after you wake up in the morning and right before you go to bed at night, commuting to and from work, your lunch hour at work, and any other moment of the day that is not filled with something that is truly valuable to your life. As you develop your time consciousness, you will uncover additional sources of incremental time. Using your natural creativity (we all have it), you should be able to think of valuable ways to use all of the incremental time you discover. Realize, however, that this is going to take a shift in your habits. It won't be easy at first. It is much easier to fill your incremental time with mindless time-wasting activities. Just try, however, for the next couple of weeks to fill it with value-added activities instead.

For example, during your commute, you might decide to listen to audio books or dictate some assignments for your assistant. This might also help reduce any traffic-related stress. Perhaps you could use your lunch break to network or complete a side project. A good way to use incremental time at home or work is to set up a "project center" with all of the tools you need to work on a particular project. Set up a desk tucked away in a corner of your house and leave a project on it. That way, it is ready and waiting for you whenever you have a few minutes to spare. If you put your mind to it, you will be able to think of other ways to use the incremental time that we otherwise take for granted. Thinking in this way will place you firmly on the path to accomplishing more than you ever thought possible - and beginning to think that maybe you actually do have enough time.

Mining for Time: Zigging Instead of Zagging

Many success commentators give the advice to "zig when others zag." That is, you are unlikely to find real success if you are doing what everyone else is doing. This is true with your time as well. If you follow the herd, you are going to continually run into crowds, lines, and traffic congestion, all of which are huge wastes of time. Do you drive to and from work the same time as everyone else? Do you go the gym right before or after work – just like everyone else? Do you go to the grocery store on Sunday afternoon along with everyone else? Do you get in line at the car wash on a hot day and wait with everyone else? Do you shop on

Black Friday so that you can get the "best deals," along with the most ferocious crowds and lines? Many people fall into these traps and never think twice about all the time they are wasting. Now, there may be very legitimate reasons why you do these things at these times. Maybe your job doesn't allow any flexibility in arrival and departure times. Maybe you just love the rush of Black Friday shopping. If you take a hard look at these and other areas, however, you can probably find a few times when you can zig while others zag. You could go to the grocery store early on Sunday morning before church, then have the rest of the day following church for family or free time. You could go to the gym later in the evening – and still watch television while you work out! This will not only save you time, but probably give you a more restful night's sleep as well. As you become more "time conscious," thinking about the best ways to use your time, you will undoubtedly think of other ways to avoid the masses and save yourself some time.

Mining for Time: Getting Bogged Down With the Little Things

It is common sense that we should focus on our more important projects, but we can't seem to help ourselves from getting bogged down with the little things. At work, we go through our emails instead of focusing on a big project. At home, we pick up around the house instead of fixing the clogged sink. There is a logical explanation for why we do this. The little things seem easier and make it feel like we are accomplishing something. This is a mindset we have to change if we are ever going to achieve greater success in life. The problem with concentrating on the little things is that the big things remain. Then we run out of time. If we knock out the big things first, we often find that many of the little things resolve themselves. Thus, we would have a net gain of time. How many times have you received a non-urgent email and then, some time later, a follow-up email indicating that the matter had already been resolved? It happens a lot for most people. In fact, a great way to save time at work is to open your email first thing in the morning, immediately respond to any emails that are absolutely critical, then completely close out of your email for a couple of hours and concentrate on your major project for the day. This will save you an inordinate amount of time as you have eliminated the temptation to look at and respond to emails every few minutes (or seconds). Establish a periodic time when you will check for other urgent email, maybe once every hour or two. After your major projects are finished for the day, you can use any remaining time to take care of those non-urgent emails. If you are an email addict, this will feel like quite the treat at the end of the day.

Regardless of whether you are at home or work, plan your day to prioritize and knock out the big projects first. You will gain more control of your life, save time in the long run, and lead a more peaceful existence as a result.

Mining for Time: Lack of Motivation and the Fears of Failure and Success

Why do we waste time? Is it fun? Sometimes, but far from always. Sure, there are those moments we really do need to "chill out" and not think about anything at all. That's healthy and we can allocate such time to relaxation, which is an important element of our lives. There are many times though when we waste an inordinate amount of time for no reason.

Lack of motivation may be a huge cause of this. How many times have you said during a particular day "I just can't get motivated to do anything"? If you stop and think about why you are not motivated, there is usually a good answer. Maybe you are physically tired. If that is the case, then find the common-sense solution to the problem. You probably need more sleep, more exercise, and less caffeine.

If we take an honest look within ourselves, we may find that we waste a lot of time out of fear. This could be the fear of failure, the fear of success, or both. What happens when one or both of these fears paralyze you? You avoid constructive use of your time and turn to the internet, video games, and television. Maybe you take it a step further and rely on even unhealthier vices to "unwind" or "take the edge off." If you continually turn to such vices as a means of distracting yourself from life, then that is a problem. At the very least, you are not making good use of your most precious commodity. At worst, you may become an addict.

Chapter 2 addressed the topics of motivation and fear. The solution is simply to take action. Once you do this, motivation and fear should no longer be problems for you. Perhaps, even after taking some action and eliminating your fear, you are still not motivated. Maybe you decide you are perfectly happy and content the way things are, including the amount of time you fritter away. That is a perfectly legitimate choice and I'm not here to argue with you. It is a choice, however, that will most likely prevent you from dominating the second half of your life.

Using Time: Creating a "Time Roadmap"

We can make the most effective use of our time by filling it, in the appropriate percentages, with the things that matter most. The best way you can figure this out is to spend some quiet time writing. This is so important because it gives you an unobstructed view of your thoughts. Our minds are filled with way too much information during the day for us to get a clear picture of our goals and priorities. It may be uncomfortable at first, but give it a try. It works!

Now, for the purposes of time management, write down the things you *want* to spend your non-sleep time on, and the desired percentages of time you want to spend on them. Keep in mind this is only a listing of your desired allocation – if you lived in a perfect world without unexpected distractions and detours. Be honest. No one has to see this list but you. In fact, you might not want to share it at all because your friends and family may be offended by the amount of time you have allocated to them! In any event, an example might look like this:

Activity	Percentage of Time	Number of Hours
Work/Career	42	50
Household Chores	8	9
Personal Chores	5	6
Time with Family	21	25
Time with Friends	7	8
Exercise/Health	6	7

Spirituality	3	4
Relaxation	8	10
Total	**100**	**119**

This example is based on 17 non-sleep hours per day, and no job-related work on the weekends. So, this hypothetical person has 119 available hours. If they spend 10 hours per weekday on job and career-related "work," including commuting and work-related social events, that is 50 hours, or 42 percent of their time. Everyone's categories and desired percentages are going to be different. Different occupations will of course require varying allocations. A teacher's categories and time will vary from an engineer's. You may think 42 percent is high or low for "Work/Career." Certainly, if you are trying to obtain a promotion or seeking a career change, you are going to have to add some percentage points to this category. Obviously, you will have to take these points away from something else.

When you write down your list and assign percentages to each category, it will likely be scary when you realize you cannot go beyond 100 percent. Spend some time working on your desired percentages. Again, these are *desired* percentages. It will be impossible to actually replicate them in real life. This list will simply be your target. It will show you how you should strive to spend your time in order to lead a fulfilling life. It will always be a work-in-progress for you to revisit. If you need to spend more time in one category, then you will have to subtract time from another category.

The next step will be both fun and a little scary. Write down how you spend your time for the next week. This is like writing down calories when you are undertaking a new diet. Live life like you normally would, but honestly record how you spend your time. This will be second nature for time-keeping lawyers. Others may be in for a real shock. After you have finished the week, compare this information with the time roadmap you created. See what adjustments you might need to make in your daily routine. Also, as mentioned above, your roadmap will be an ever-changing work-in-progress. Your career may need 60 percent of your time one year and only 40 percent the next.

Using Time: Prioritizing

You can and should prioritize your time on an hourly, daily, weekly, monthly, and annual basis. This sounds like a real chore if you are not used to doing it. It will be at first. As you gain time-consciousness, however, this process will become easier and easier.

Begin by prioritizing your specific activities. You can and should do this not only on a daily basis, but for longer periods of time as well. For example, on Sunday evening, you may write down your list of priorities for the week and review your previous week's list to see how you fared. As for daily planning, try not to let the actual planning take too much of your time. You know what needs to be done. Take a few moments in the morning to jot down your goals for the day, placing stars or otherwise emphasizing the ones that absolutely need to be accomplished. These are the top priorities that you will work on first, with the possibility of one exception, as discussed below.

As you prioritize your activities, consider when you work best. Most of us are either "morning people" or "night owls." Whichever one you are, you know that you operate at a higher level during your special part of the day. Shouldn't you perform really important activities during that time period? While it may not be feasible to work on a job-related project late in the evening, you can at least dedicate that time to something that is really important to your life. If, after reading this book, you decide that your number one current goal is to get in great shape, and you are a night owl, perhaps you should dedicate time late in the evening to working out. If you are a morning person who wants to write a book, then dedicate time first thing in the morning to writing.

Prioritizing time generally comes down to one question: "what is the best possible use of my time right now?" Let that question guide you, and the answer will help you in many aspects of your personal and professional development.

Using Time: Time Consciousness

The more you practice time management skills, the more you will notice other areas of your life where you can spend time more efficiently. This is called time consciousness and it is your gateway to greater success. If you have not been very time conscious to this point, you can and should change that now. While it is difficult to break habits, the good news is that new habits become easier and easier with the passage of time. The first few days are the hardest, but you will get exponentially better at practicing time consciousness. Before you know it, you will be teaching others about it.

An added benefit to becoming more time conscious is that you will naturally devote less time to feeling sad, anxious, jealous, and/or depressed. This book is not intended to address those issues, although positive thinking and mindfulness (attentive awareness of the present moment) are certainly recurrent themes. Moreover, if you follow the advice in this book, you will quickly realize that negative thoughts and emotions will never in a million years take you where you want or need to go. They certainly won't lead to fulfillment. Thus, you won't want to waste any more time dwelling on them.

Finally, a note of caution. As you become more time conscious, remember to always keep in mind other people's feelings. If you operate effectively and efficiently, you may appear rude to some segment of the population. This is something you have to learn to balance. While you can't control what others think about you, and you certainly can't please everyone, there are some things you can control. You can stay present when you are with others and show genuine interest in them, making sure your time together is quality time. Time management, like life itself, is a balancing act. Practice every day and you will see great results.

Questions to Ponder

1. How much time do you spend with electronic entertainment (including television and the internet) out of sheer boredom?

2. What areas of your life do you have idle time that seems like it is just being wasted?

3.   How could you better use your commute and other areas of incremental time that is otherwise wasted?

4.   Is there a project you could work on during your idle time?

4 DOMINATE YOUR CAREER

The crowning fortune of a man is to be born to some pursuit which finds him employment and happiness, whether it be to make baskets, or broadswords, or canals, or statues, or songs.

- Ralph Waldo Emerson

Who's Looking Out for Us?

Generation X has been criticized for its lack of loyalty and tendency to job-hop. A closer look at these traits, however, reveals validity in our generation's way of thinking. Employers are running businesses, not humanitarian efforts. Like it or not, we are only useful for a finite period of time that may or may not last the lengths of our careers. This is not meant to be a harsh statement. In times of great economic surplus, it is easy to believe that our employers care for us in the same sense that family members care for each other. No matter how great an employer is, however, employment can never truly be guaranteed. Circumstances can and do change and, with that, there may be a reduced or no need for employees.

In today's economic environment, most of us recognize that we may or may not have our current jobs five years from now. A change in our employment circumstances may or may not be of our own choosing. Prior generations were much more likely to be "company" men and women, working for one employer their entire careers and retiring with a nice pension, a gold watch, and a pat on the back. In general, employees were rewarded for loyal and faithful service to their employers. Somewhere along the way, however, it became painfully obvious that the loyalty did not run both ways. When the economy or other considerations dictated, companies had no reluctance in laying off employees, even those from whom they had received many years of loyal service. Generation X members watched this happen to their parents. Thus, we asked a simple question. If employers were not going to be loyal to us, then why would we, as a generation, wed ourselves to our employers?

Attention span, or lack thereof, has also likely played a role in our generation's attitude towards employment. We grew up with hundreds of television channels, computers, and video games. Stimulating entertainment has never been far away. Certainly, this contributes to our desire to look for the "next big thing" in life, such as a more exciting or higher paying job.

Let's be clear about one thing, however. When we talk about Generation X's lack of loyalty to employers, we are not talking about laziness or poor performance. Indeed, our generation has proven that the "slacker" label previous generations used to describe us was misplaced. Generation X employees work just as hard as anyone else, but we do it with the underlying sentiment that working for multiple employers (or eventually striking out on our own) will not only be preferable, but likely a necessity.

This two-way lack of loyalty could be perceived as a bad thing. It is much better, however, to treat it as a positive. Sure, realizing that our employers are not overly loyal to us is a scary thought. After all, who wouldn't love the security of knowing that they have a job for life? We can spend our time worrying about this lack of security, or we can develop a deeper appreciation that it is actually a blessing in disguise. The fact that we cannot depend upon lasting employment forces us to adapt and to become the absolute best we can be. Thank goodness our generation is known for being self-reliant.

At this stage in your career, how do you feel about it? Is it a means to an end (i.e., it pays the bills)? Do you love what you do so much that you feel like you don't even work? Are you somewhere in between? Whatever your current situation, unless you are already independently wealthy and/or retired, your career is a major component of your life and overall well-being. Let's take a look to see if perhaps there are some halftime adjustments you need to make. The rest of this chapter is devoted to time-tested techniques you can use to dominate the second part of your career, regardless of whether you are working for someone else, running your own business, or looking to make a radical change. Yes, some of this is "Careers 101" stuff. If you are like me, you can always use some refresher training – and you may have slacked off in recent years. Others may not have devoted much time to developing their careers at all. In either case, this may be your last best chance to avoid becoming the 65-year-old taking orders from the 25-year-old.

Doing What You Love

Time and work flow effortlessly when you love what you do. You know the feeling – you've experienced it at different times in your life. So, at this stage, you need to ask yourself a critical question. Are you doing what you love for a living? If not, do you at least *like* what you do? If the answer is "yes," then the remaining concepts in this chapter will be much easier for you to tackle. What if the answer is no?

Think about what it feels like as you prepare for and go to work each day. If it is something you dread and have negative feelings about, do you want to spend the rest of your life feeling this way? Of course not. So, first, take the opportunity to figure out exactly what causes your negative feelings. It could be your co-workers or boss. If that is the case, and you have explored methods of resolving the issue without success, then maybe it is time to move your career elsewhere. That will, of course, take some extra work, but your happiness is worth the price.

It could be your actual work that is the problem. That's a big problem, but not an unsolvable one. If you dislike what you do for a living, you need to take a long hard look at where you envision the rest of your career heading. Is your current occupation what you want to be doing when you retire? On the day you die? If it's not, then what would you like to be doing? Is there a career you would like to have, but believe your present circumstances make it impossible? The process of figuring all of this out may take some time, but again it is well worth the investment.

The next step in the process is to start thinking about change by carving out a little time for yourself with no one else around – no co-workers, no clients or customers, no friends, and no family. There is no obligation in just thinking. Grab a laptop or a pen and paper. Start writing out what you had originally envisioned for yourself, where you see your current career headed, and your ultimate career goal. It is crucial that you actually write. Simply thinking about these things is not the same. You will be amazed that, when you actually start writing down your thoughts, feelings come out that you never realized you had. When you undertake this process, be completely honest and don't be embarrassed about what you are writing. No one else ever has to see this. Maybe a few hours won't be enough. That's okay. Keep working at it periodically. You and your ultimate career satisfaction should be your number one priority. The process may take months, a year, or even longer. If you are having trouble with this process, or need inspiration, Dr. Ken Robinson has written an excellent book titled *Finding Your Element*. It's all about figuring out exactly what you want to do with your life – no matter how old you are. Eventually, after spending enough time with your thoughts, you will have a firm grasp of your true ambitions. You may even find yourself surprised at the results.

Now comes the hard part. You've figured out that you want to be doing something slightly or even completely different than what you are doing now. Unfortunately, you have bills, a family, and other responsibilities. This is when you have to decide how badly you want a change in your career. Napoleon Hill states in *Think and Grow Rich* that, if your desire for something is strong enough, you will stop at nothing to get it. This is undoubtedly true. Need proof? Think of any difficult achievement in your life. At a certain point, you willed yourself to accomplish it. You could have quit. You didn't. You simply would not accept "no" for an answer. You can accomplish this same result on a larger scale. Recall the story of Tim at the beginning of the book. The problem with most people is that they think or dream about what they want, but never actually take any action to get it. If you truly want to make a change in your career, you will find a way to accomplish that change. It may mean working or studying at night and on the weekends until you can transition away from your current position. It may mean cutting back on television, social media, and other forms of entertainment so you have time to work on your new endeavor. It may mean accepting lower pay and cutting expenses. There will undoubtedly be sacrifices. Again, however, your long-term happiness is worth the price.

One of my friends was enjoying a tremendous career in the corporate world. She received countless promotions and assumed many leadership roles, all enough to make her peers somewhat envious I'm sure – and all by the time she reached her mid-thirties. But she was an entrepreneur at heart, and had been developing several businesses in her spare time, all while juggling family responsibilities and excelling at her day job. She came to a point where she knew that, if she was going to achieve all that she wanted to achieve in her entrepreneurial ventures, she would have to part ways with her employer. Talk about risk. Goodbye steady paycheck and 401(k). Hello limitless possibilities! She had made a halftime adjustment – at a time when most people would say that is too scary or impossible. She paid a tremendous price for this radical change in her life, in the form of risk and facing her fears. She is doing great in her second career, however, and has found the place she was always destined to be.

If you are not willing to pay the price for a particular change, then you are making a decision about what you value. It could be that you value watching television and relaxing more than you value making a major life change. That's perfectly okay. Just recognize that it is a decision *you* are making. We often ignore the fact that we are making an endless stream of choices in life, and instead we blame our circumstances on luck and just wait for better things to happen. Every moment presents a choice if you really pause to think about it. Keep reading or stop reading? Stick with my diet or break it? Pursue my dream another day or procrastinate? One bad habit I have personally worked to overcome is to change my thinking from whether I *can* accomplish something to whether I *want* to accomplish it *badly* enough. Try it. Instead of thinking in terms of possible versus impossible, or lucky versus unlucky, try thinking in terms of a simple question: "how badly do I want it?" Do you want an exotic sports car? Sure, many of us do, in the sense that we would gladly take one right now and never look back. But do you *really* want it? Are you willing to forsake all your hobbies, take some risks, and work from dusk until dawn to get one? Maybe, but for most people, the answer is probably "no." You *can* have it – you just don't *want* it *badly* enough. The same goes with making a drastic career change. If you truly want to make a change, you will go to any length to accomplish that change. If you have decided you are willing to do that, then you simply start the process by taking your first small step forward. That initial action will create motivation and more action, which will help you build momentum until you eventually accomplish your goal.

Establishing Your Personal Brand Internally

Maybe you already have a career you love, are not yet ready to make a major change, or are in the process of making a change. Whatever your present career circumstances, you still have to make a living. If we are going to be working anyway, we might as well do it to the best of our ability and be successful. This is easier said than done when we consider what we have learned as a generation. We know that our employers are not necessarily loyal to us, even if we are excellent employees. What can we do to minimize risk and to become so indispensable that we can't be thrown away? First and foremost, we need to develop our own personal brand. We need to become "famous" as our own entities. You want to be known as you – a separate and valuable commodity - not "Employee # 116 at XYZ Company." This may sound like beginner advice and it is. I'm willing to bet, however, that many of us have gotten complacent or brushed this goal aside in order to concentrate on other areas of life, such as raising our children. Still others may have never started in the first place, perhaps because of multiple career changes.

The first step to establishing your own brand is to become well-known within your own organization. We absolutely must perform at a high level for our employers. This is why we are being compensated in the first place. That is not how you truly set yourself part, however. Beyond doing good work, you need to take steps to make yourself indispensable. There are several ways to differentiate yourself in this regard: (1) *actively* participating in your workplace; (2) taking on challenging assignments; and (3) becoming a leader within your organization.

Simply *participating with enthusiasm* in the workplace will position you ahead of most of your co-workers. Most people go to work, keep their heads down, hope that no one notices them, then go home. This is a serviceable approach, but not one that will really get you ahead. Participate in meetings, attend social events, and get out of your office regularly to interact with others in your organization, especially those whom you normally wouldn't. Relationships are the key to life. Becoming visible in your workplace will help establish you as a team player, as someone who is genuinely interested in your organization and colleagues, and as someone whom others will want to keep around.

Moreover, there is a purely selfish reason to participate in the workplace - it makes life more interesting. Make your work experience more enjoyable and, at the very least, your time at work will pass more quickly. Too often in life, we resist the present moment in our heads, focusing instead on thinking that some point in the future will be better. At work, we tend to do this by refusing to participate, putting forth minimal effort, and keeping to ourselves. This is like our own little mental rebellion. We don't want to be at work, so we'll show them! The problem with this approach is obvious – we are also hurting ourselves. Our internal resistance creates a vicious cycle where work really does become a negative experience. First, we tell ourselves in our heads that it is going to be negative. Then, we perpetuate the cycle with our mental resistance. Instead, try acknowledging that you have to be at work anyway, so you might as well make the most of your time there. It doesn't cost you a dime and will make your life immensely more enjoyable. Moreover, it will place you well on your way to dominating the remainder of your career.

Another way to become indispensable at work is to take on the challenging assignments that everyone else refuses. Without the aid of extreme good luck, you will never become all you can be in life without breaking out of your comfort zone. Taking on difficult assignments is a scary idea. After all, who wants to fail? Fear of failure is one of the most debilitating fears, especially as it relates to your career. It is a fear you must cast aside and eliminate on a permanent basis. Once your mind is liberated from the fear of failure, and you become comfortable being uncomfortable, you can soar to great heights. Besides, supervisors generally realize that the difficult assignments are difficult. Thus, they will typically be a little more forgiving if your results are something less than perfect. This fact alone should help alleviate any remaining fear you have. While somewhat scary, challenging assignments are your quickest path to growth. You will never know how much you can accomplish if you keep doing the things you already know how to do. Taking on novel or challenging assignments will only make you stronger. This will make you an asset to your employer, and more marketable to potential employers, should the need for a new position arise.

Last, but certainly not least, if you want to stand out in your organization and in life, become a leader. If you were running a business, consider who would be more indispensable to you: a leader or a follower? Followers can be found anywhere but leaders are rare. If you can develop into a good leader for your company, you will become indispensable. The company will always make a place for leaders, even as trends come and go. If your department gets phased out, but you have established yourself as a leader, the company will do everything in its power to keep you. You may be thinking to yourself "how can I become a leader when I work in a lower-level position?" Leadership does not depend upon a job title or placement within a company. Everyone has the potential to be a leader. You may become a leader of your fellow employees by communicating with them, listening to them, and helping them with their problems. Your supervisors will recognize you as a leader when you speak up, take on difficult tasks, and offer suggestions and ideas to improve processes at work. After you have read this chapter, and the chapter on leadership, if you are interested in further study, there are many excellent volumes devoted to the topic, including those listed in the *Recommended Reading* appendix. Indeed, like many of the subjects in this book, leadership is something that you can constantly improve, but will never truly master. If you think you are not a born leader, that may be true, but it does not mean that you cannot become a great leader over time. If you want to truly set yourself apart at work, and dominate the second half of your career, start becoming a leader today.

Becoming a Portable Commodity

In addition to developing our personal brand or identity for internal job security, we must be mindful that even the very best employees cannot be guaranteed job security. The post-2008 economy has made this readily apparent. There are Ivy League-educated bankers and lawyers looking for work. Top sales professionals have had to undergo drastic career changes to make ends meet. These realities confirm that, even if we are the best of the best, that may not matter if the company goes under, there is no longer a need for our specific services, or we get laid off for economic reasons.

Consequently, we should always be working to develop our external visibility. Should circumstances warrant, we need to make sure we are attractive to other employers. We need to be "portable" and able to transplant our careers into another company. Do other employers know about us? If not, they should and we need to work to make that happen. This is accomplished in relatively simple ways: (1) making sure we have attractive bios; (2) writing and speaking in our areas of expertise; and (3) networking with others so that they know we exist.

As the years roll by, it is easy to lose track of your accomplishments, especially if you become comfortable with your current employer. If you like and enjoy your present position, you may feel like you don't need to keep your bio updated. You do. Things always change. That is an undeniable truth. You need to keep track of your career accomplishments, experience, certifications, speaking engagements, writings, media appearances, and awards. Keeping these items in a nice, organized, readily-accessible format will make it easy for you to explain to a potential employer on short notice how much value you can truly bring to their organization.

Writing and speaking are both highly effective methods for getting your brand out there and making sure you are a portable commodity. Write and speak in your areas of specialty to let others know about your expertise. Want clients to hire you for an area in which you lack experience? Start writing and speaking about that subject. The best way to learn is to teach others. If you don't consider yourself a good writer or speaker, or you just don't like doing those things, there are certainly other methods for increasing the value of your brand. Don't give up hope just because you may need improvement. As with most things in life, you will improve by leaps and bounds with a little practice.

Finally, don't forget the simple act of networking when trying to establish your brand externally. How are people going to know about you if you don't spend time with them? The next chapter is all about building better relationships and networking, so after reading it, you'll be all set to effectively spread the word about your brand.

Becoming Specialized – But Not Too Specialized

People generally hire experts, not generalists. So, whatever your career, work hard to develop a specialty and become known for something. Your life will become infinitely easier if people seek you out for your services instead of you seeking them out to sell them something. In addition to becoming specialized, you should also endeavor to develop alternative marketable skills – a "backup plan," so to speak. Jack Welch, famed leadership author, and the former CEO of General Motors, advised others to "change before you have to." Great advice, as history is littered with thousands of examples of people and companies who had initial success and then failed because they refused to change with the times. As mentioned above, the current economic climate has left highly-educated and highly-skilled professionals out on the streets looking for work. Times change. Services that are in demand now may not be in demand ten years from now. Therefore, it is never a bad idea to branch out and acquire new skills. If there are innovations on the horizon in your industry, study them now so that you can change with the times. Consider starting an online business. Learn about something totally outside of your current field. The bottom line is that you should be constantly expanding your skill set and challenging yourself – that's what makes a rich and rewarding life anyway. Then, if you are left without a job in your current industry, you will at least have something to fall back on, instead of being forced to look for work as an unskilled laborer.

Developing an Entrepreneurial Spirit

Whether working for someone else or yourself, an entrepreneurial spirit is absolutely critical. Service will only get you so far. You have to be able to develop new business for yourself or your employer. How do you do that? By thinking like an entrepreneur. Even if you do not have an ownership stake in your employer's business, act like you do. This will help you add value and become indispensable. That is certainly a worthwhile goal. After all, you certainly *do* have an ownership interest in yourself.

Entrepreneurs brainstorm for new ideas and look for opportunities. If you have ideas for improving the business, share them. They may or may not be accepted, but your desire to add value will certainly be recognized. The best ideas usually begin with something you think of that will make your life easier but that doesn't already exist. Imagine yourself in the shoes of your clients and brainstorm ideas that will make their lives easier.

Entrepreneurs think outside the box. They are not satisfied with the way things are. They look for new ways to solve problems. They look for better ways. How will you differentiate yourself from your competitor? By doing the same things they do? No - you will look for a more innovative approach – something that will set you apart. Your ideas may seem crazy. Maybe they are. But remember that most great inventions and accomplishments started as crazy ideas. Develop a "horseless carriage"? Crazy idea. The television? Crazy. The internet? Forget about it – that's totally crazy! Become comfortable with crazy ideas and you may just find your greatest success.

Entrepreneurs are risk-takers. Our willingness to accept risk plays a key role in our attainment of great success. Not haphazard risk, but calculated risk. Entrepreneurs, leaders, and successful people in general take calculated risks. They do their research and try to focus their energy on risks that are likely to pay off. If you have played it safe to this point in your career, you know about what you can expect if you continue to do the same thing. If you are risk averse, that probably means a moderate amount of success. If you want to attain the next level of success during the second half of your career, start becoming comfortable with exiting your comfort zone and taking some risks.

Keeping Up With Technology and Social Media

Fortunately, Generation X is very comfortable with technology. As we continue to age, however, there will come a point where changes in technology will happen so fast that we become frustrated or even fearful of them. After all, technological changes are exponential in nature. We cannot even imagine what will happen over the next 40 to 50 years. It is downright scary. It is also alarming to think about what will happen to us if we don't keep pace with these changes. Resolve with me right now to never let that happen.

If you are not currently using the internet and social media to enhance your brand, you are already behind in the game, but it is certainly not too late. In fact, you must start now because the internet and social media are integral parts of any brand, including yours. Perform an internet search on your name. If you do not appear on the first page of the results, you are basically nonexistent in the virtual world. How can you change this? Start by getting yourself "out there" on the internet. Blogs, vlogs, and social media posts will enhance your visibility. Consider starting a career-related blog or vlog. Consider starting a non-career-related blog or vlog. The more activity you engage in online, the more likely search engines are to acknowledge your existence.

Don't think of social media and the internet as marketing tools, however. You are unlikely to attract clients simply by being active online. Instead, use these tools primarily for networking with others. This means actively using them and doing the same thing you would with regular networking – being genuine and adding value – not deliberately shilling your product or service.

When you achieve something, work with your company's marketing department (if it has one) to see if a press release can be issued about your accomplishment. This is a great way to enhance your visibility as it will usually result in multiple search results associated with your name. If you don't have access to a marketing department, contact the media on your own to see if they might be interested in running a story about you. This can be a win-win. The media needs news and you need publicity. So, don't be afraid of contacting them. Hate the idea of self-promotion? Keep reading.

Don't Be Afraid of Self-Promotion

Self-promotion is often preceded by the word "shameless" and viewed as something we should not be doing. In this increasingly-competitive modern world, however, self-promotion is not only desirable, it is a necessity. You just have to make sure it is *tactful* self-promotion and not *shameless* self-promotion. No one else is going to invest much time promoting you. So, you are going to have to do it and become comfortable doing it. Don't be afraid to let others, both internal and external to your organization, know what you have accomplished. How is publishing an article going to benefit you if no one knows about it? The fact is your employer wants to know about these things. You should be communicating to your company exactly what you are doing to add value in your chosen field. Likewise, you should let your external network know about your accomplishments. This is easier than ever to accomplish with social media. As with many things, however, the language you use makes all the difference. There is a clear difference between bragging and showing genuine excitement for accomplishing something. Consider the following alternative social media posts: (A) "Won Regional Manager of the Year Award Last Night – that makes three years in a row!" vs. (B) "Honored XYZ chose me as Regional Manager of the Year. I couldn't have done it without such a great team." Of course, you will always rub *someone* the wrong way with your posts. If you are being tactful and not boastful, the problem will be theirs, not yours.

Periodically Analyzing Whether You Are Moving Forward

Every once in awhile, perhaps once or twice per year, schedule some time with yourself. Get out that laptop or pen and paper. Write down what you have accomplished during the preceding time period. Remember that no one ever has to see this but you. Consider whether there were things you wanted to accomplish but didn't. Consider whether you are moving forward in your career, stagnating, or falling behind. Life moves very quickly and, before we know it, years pass and we find that we have stopped improving or, worse, proceeded down the entirely wrong career path. This is why some time alone with your thoughts and a writing instrument is so important. It allows you to consider where you have been, where you appear to be headed, and to make necessary adjustments to your direction. This quality time alone with your thoughts is the best investment you can make. If there is one person in the world you should want to invest in, it is yourself. Unfortunately, this is the one person we most often overlook. Don't let that happen anymore!

Front-Loading Your Work

As you have read through this chapter, you may have thought "yes, I agree, but who can devote so much time and energy to their career?" The chapters on time management and work-life balance will certainly help. But this is as good a place as any to discuss front-loading your work. This means doing more work at the beginning, then making adjustments and taking a breather later. You don't always have to exert 100 percent of your energy on every aspect of life. Instead, simply recognize that doing more work at the beginning pays more dividends than playing from behind. For example, consider first impressions. If you demonstrate early on your commitment to become a leader and your willingness to tackle difficult assignments, that will become your reputation even if, later on, circumstances dictate that you have to slow down a little, or pass over some assignments. Your reputation will already have been created and you will have a little leeway for establishing that ever elusive work-life balance. While your reputation can certainly be eroded, it will take more than a couple incidents for that to happen. If you have already cemented a great reputation, your employer will love you and will give you much greater flexibility than someone who has not done the same things. As another example of front-loading, consider your workweek. If you work really hard Monday and Tuesday, you gain control of your work and can afford to relax a little later in the week. If you come in late Monday morning and devote less than your best effort, you typically end up playing from behind the rest of the week and have to work really hard to try to get back to even. So, work hard early so you can afford to take a break later.

Questions to Ponder

1. Do you have a sense of dread as you head to work in the morning?

2. Do you enjoy your work environment?

3. Do you get satisfaction from your work?

4. Are you doing what you would be doing if money was not a concern?

5. What did you think you would be doing by this point in your life?

6. Do you really want to make a change in your career, such that you are willing to do anything to accomplish that change?

7. What three things could you begin to do that would set you apart from others?

8. What is your "plan B" if something were to happen to your current career?

5 THE WORK LIFE BALANCE CONUNDRUM

Be moderate in order to taste the joys of life in abundance.

- Epicurus

Is Work-Life Balance a Myth?

Authors, bloggers, and other commentators have been discussing and dissecting the issue of work-life balance for years. No one has arrived at the formula for achieving the coveted balance. The modern trend seems to suggest that there is no such thing as work-life balance because something has to give. This theory makes a lot of intuitive sense. Many people's definition of work-life balance is being the best at everything. If that is your goal, you are going to be extremely disappointed. We know that, primarily because of the limits on our time and energy, we are not going to be the best at everything. We cannot be the best at our jobs, the best spouse, the best parent, and the best friend all at the same time. Something has to give. So, if you are looking for absolute perfection in everything you do, you are experiencing quite the conundrum. Instead of looking for perfection in yourself, consider recognizing that the idealized concept of work-life balance is what is flawed. This chapter presents two alternative approaches that will allow you to have a realistic work-life balance, and hopefully make you a happier person overall. The first approach is to figure out what your priorities are, and then weight the activities in your life toward your priorities. If you are doing what you value more, then you should enjoy a happier, less stressed existence. The second approach is to practice "work-life integration," which simply means that you don't need to balance anything because all of your activities, even your work, are things you enjoy. This approach is a bit trickier, because work makes up a large percentage of our lives. Keep reading, however, and you may just find that this is the approach for you. The chapter concludes with a brief discussion on health and wellness, which, no matter the method you use to balance your life, should be a major priority for you. After all, what good is work-life balance if you are not around to enjoy it?

What Balance Do You Want?

Your ideal work-life balance is not the same as mine. The absolute first step is to figure out what you want. If you are reading this book, you probably have experienced enough of life to have some idea of what you want to get out of it. Surprisingly, however, a large percentage of the adult population still has no clue. They are just sleepwalking through life, waiting for that moment in the future when everything will fall into place. The problem is, that moment will never happen on its own. You have to work to make it happen. You can start by doing something that people rarely, if ever, do. Get out your pen and paper, or a laptop, and take some notes – notes for your use only. Write down your goals, priorities, and desires for your life. Write down everything that comes to mind: your ambitions, the people and things that are most important to you, the places you want to go, and the experiences you want to have. This may take some time but, with practice, you will realize things about yourself that you never would have without writing them down. Our heads are too filled with a million other thoughts every day that we rarely, if ever, take the time to make a cohesive list of our goals and priorities.

While you are writing things down, ask yourself what your main current priority is, as well as your main or overriding goal in life? An example of a top current priority may be to adopt a strict but feasible exercise and nutrition program. Or it may be to obtain a promotion at work. Examples of overriding lifetime goals may be to create your own successful business, become CEO of a company, or retire to the beach. Many will be tempted to adopt an overriding life goal of being the best parent possible. That is fine, but realize that every parent wants to be the best parent possible. And we all are. We all make the best decisions possible for raising our children, whether that means staying at home or working outside of the home. We wouldn't have it any other way. There will come a time, however, when our children leave us and go out on their own. We will still have plenty of our own lives left. So, please consider what is *your* overriding goal for *yourself* in life. This is not selfish. You owe it to yourself, your family, and your friends to use this one lifetime to be everything you can possibly be. It may take you a year or more to decide what your overriding goal is, but you will know it when you think of it, and it will be worth your time and energy. So keep thinking!

Once you have determined your overriding goal in life, make sure you give regular attention to that goal. It may not command the most attention daily, but make sure you are always moving towards it. If you don't, then you are going to end up feeling very unfulfilled. Decide what small daily steps you can take towards your goal, whether that means saving fifty cents – or planning for fifteen minutes – each and every day. Then, make sure you allocate enough time to your other important goals and priorities. The following sections will help you prioritize that time effectively.

Revisiting Time Consciousness

In the chapter on time management, you learned to make valuable use of your time and to become "time conscious," meaning you continually ask yourself whether you are making the best use of your time. You force yourself to do this consciously at first but it eventually becomes subconscious through repetition. This is extremely important for helping to create a greater feeling of work-life balance.

Quality Time

Having a great work-life balance has more to do with what is going on in your head than it does with the actual amount of time you spend on each activity. Unfortunately, this is an area where we all have difficulty. The countless thoughts running through our heads create way too much mental noise and we are always thinking about all the things we need to do, or where we are going next. When we are at home, we are thinking about work. When we are at work, we are thinking about home. This creates quite a mess in our heads.

We all need to work towards spending quality time with everything we do. This requires practice, dedication, and significant mental energy. It can never truly be mastered. It is a skill that you can become really good at over time. Quality time means that you are "present," "mindful," or "awake" for each activity in your life. You are not "zoning out," imagining you were somewhere else, worrying about the hundred tasks you need to complete in the coming week, or glued to your electronic device.

We all spend a lot of time at work, there is no question about that. Be honest with yourself and consider how much of that time is actually quality work time. How much time do you spend gossiping with co-workers, going to get coffee, taking extended lunch breaks, surfing the internet, or daydreaming? These activities all have their place in life, at least to some extent. If you do these things and still have to take work home in the evening or on the weekends, you have to stop and think whether these frivolous activities are actually robbing you of precious time elsewhere, such as with your family or friends.

Some of us have jobs where the length of time we spend at work is dependent upon how efficiently we can process all of the tasks we have to complete. If we get done at 4:00 p.m., we can leave. If we don't get done until 7:00 p.m., then we have to work until then. If your job is like this, then you have a tremendous opportunity to work smarter and more efficiently, and then leave work and turn your attention to other areas.

If, in contrast, you have the type of job where you *have* to be at your desk a certain number of hours regardless of how busy you are, then you will have to find more creative ways to make sure all of your time is quality time. Perhaps you can take care of other business or aspects of your life during downtime at work (if, of course, this is permitted by your employer).

You may also have a job where you have to work like crazy for a period of time, followed by a period of inactivity. Anyone involved in any type of craftsmanship, legislative service, tax work, or event production may have unbalanced periods of time like this. The key is to use each period of time for its intended use. Work when you have to work. Rest and spend time with your family and friends during the off-cycles.

Just like with work, your time with family and friends should be quality time. We may wish for more quantity, but that is not the answer. Quality is the answer. You can spend 24/7 with your children, but it will not be quality time. In contrast, if you only get a couple of hours per day with them, and you make it quality time where you are truly engaged and present, then that time is infinitely more valuable than a 24 hour period filled mostly with disengagement.

That brings us to a touchy subject: electronic devices. Again, I'm not demonizing them. Our smartphones and tablets are great and can truly be life-savers. Unfortunately, however, they have created a generation of people who are not present – they are always somewhere else. Perhaps wishing they were with someone else. Perhaps just zoned out. Regardless of where they are in their minds, they are not present in the moment. Groups of friends going out to lunch where they all proceed to stare at their phones is becoming all too common in modern society. Take a look around the next time you are at a restaurant. Those people are physically present, but their minds are somewhere else. That is not quality time.

Think about your own use of electronic devices. Then, consider scaling back. You don't have to stop carrying them. Just take little breaks. If you find it exceedingly difficult, then you may have a little addiction on your hands. Thankfully, it is not a chemical addiction, so you can easily break it. Start out small. Leave your phone at the office the next time you go to lunch. You will find that you enjoy the lunch, and your company, more. Take a break from social media for one day. Then two days. Resolve to check your social media sites once per day instead of every few minutes. These suggestions may be difficult to implement at first, but you will notice that you don't miss the constant attachment nearly as much as you thought you would. You will find you can get all of the beneficial use of social media in less time.

Now certainly all of this quality time and engagement can be mentally draining (especially for introverts). You do not have to give 100 percent all the time. You must set aside time for yourself, whatever activity - or inactivity - that may be. Rest and relaxation are important parts of every day and should never be overlooked. If you are too busy on a particular day for some rest, force yourself to do it. This is very difficult, but make yourself take 15 minutes off. It will be well worth it and enable you to be less stressed and more productive overall.

Work-Life Integration

Depending upon your current career, work-life integration may be quite difficult. Essentially, this theory states that, if you enjoy what you do for a living, you simply integrate your work time with your personal time. If you already love your job, great. If not, it is not too late to get into a field that you truly love. You may be thinking that is impossible. You have a family to support. You are too far into your present career. These are certainly obstacles, but they don't make a career change impossible. As discussed in the last chapter, if you want a career change more than you want anything else, you can find a way to make it happen. If you truly believe there is no way to make a drastic career change, however, there is another way.

That other way is through the power of your mind. Stop resisting reality. Accept it. Embrace it. Make the most of every day. Find one small part of your job and truly master it. Do it for your own internal satisfaction. Then move on to another part and master it as well. Stop resisting work and relish it as a golden opportunity that some will never even have. Enjoy your co-workers, even the ones that drive you crazy. You can resist or accept things. Resistance brings a vicious cycle of negative feelings that repeats itself. Acceptance brings peace and ultimately happiness because you are no longer wasting mental energy on resistance.

Once you are either gainfully employed in a career that you love, or have at least found a way to embrace your present circumstances, then you are ready to begin practicing work-life integration. This means there are no more tidy segments of time devoted to work, friends, family, and play. You intermingle all parts of your life all the time. It may mean being closer friends with your work colleagues. It may mean leaving work early (if you can) to attend your child's recital or sporting event, then spending a couple of hours working in the evening. It may mean using your lunch hour for exercise, then staying an extra hour at the office later in the day. The main ingredient to making this work, however, is no surprise. It is your mind. It is enjoying each aspect of your day. It is not worrying about when you will get all of your work done so you can enjoy your personal time. It is being present for each moment of your life and realizing that the present moment is all you ever have, so you might as well enjoy it. That's work-life integration. When done correctly, you will find it is a beautiful thing.

Health & Wellness

Why a section on health and wellness? The answer is easy. You can't dominate the rest of your life if you are not around to do it. Unfortunately, our generation is accustomed to an infinite number of unhealthy influences. We grew up with fast food restaurants on just about every street in America, convenience and junk foods galore at the grocery store, and a proliferation of every type of sugary drink imaginable, including so-called "sports" drinks. To complement our limitless options for unhealthy eating, we have grown up with numerous entertainment options as well, including computers, video games, and hundreds of television channels from which to choose. This has been a deadly combination, leading to obesity, diabetes, and other health problems.

We can get away with unhealthy habits for a while, but there comes a time when they have to stop. That time is now. You know whether you are leading a healthy lifestyle. All of the other advice in this book is meaningless if you don't take care of yourself. While many millions of dollars are spent each year on magic formulas and diets, there is no real secret. You create a healthy lifestyle through diet and exercise.

Fad diets come and go. This book is not going to provide you with the hot new diet plan. What it will do is provide you with some universal truths about diet and nutrition. No one can deny the following: (1) moderation is key; (2) we typically eat too much and can afford to cut back on portion sizes; (3) if you want to lose weight, it is all a matter of numbers - you must burn more calories than you consume; (4) we need to drink plenty of water; and (5) we consume way too much sugar and sodium.

If you have already adopted an exercise routine, great, stick with that. If not, then you absolutely must get started. A common refrain is that we don't have time to exercise. You can rest assured, however, that you won't have time for anything in the future if you don't make time for exercise now. In that regard, it is the most important activity of your day. It should be given top priority. If the only way you can make that happen is to exercise first thing in the morning, then that is what you have to do. If you have done this before, you know that the rest of your day will come much easier if you have started out strong by exercising.

Finally, an important component of wellness is rest. Various studies have shown that seven hours of sleep per night is about optimum for most adults. Eight hours is okay. More than that is not a good sign. If you are having trouble adopting a regular sleep schedule, consider natural solutions instead of sleep aids. Are you using multiple cups of coffee or energy drinks to get going everyday, and then relying on sleep aids to go to sleep every night? It doesn't take a doctor to tell you this may not be the healthiest of routines. Try cutting back to one cup of coffee, which, after a couple of days, you will find still gives you a great "pick-me-up." It will also allow you to naturally fall asleep at night. Evening exercise may be a good way to help you fall asleep even easier. Your body will be tired and begging for sleep. Plus, the exercise will have helped burn off any residual stress from your day – stress that would have otherwise kept you awake.

Questions to Ponder

1. Does your life feel balanced? If not, what areas feel unbalanced?

2. Are you truly "present" in life, or are you "sleepwalking" through life and/or always thinking about what happened in the past or things you need to do in the future?

3. Do you spend quality time in all areas of your life, including work?

4.   Are you time conscious and avoid wasting valuable time?

5.   Is your perceived lack of balance really dissatisfaction with some area of your life? If so, what can you do to change that?

6.   Have you made wellness a top priority? If not, why?

6 LEAD FUTURE GENERATIONS TO SUCCESS

If your actions inspire others to dream more, learn more, do more, and become more, you are a leader.

- John Quincy Adams

Why Become a Leader?

If you are a member of Generation X, odds are you are already a leader, regardless of whether you want to be. You may be a coach. You may be a leader among friends. If you have kids, you are a leader for them. When it comes to your career, you may have worked your way into some type of leadership position. Whether you have or not, and regardless of your current title, you should want to develop your leadership ability because, quite simply, leadership is the number one gateway to greater success. Continually developing your leadership skills will benefit you in all aspects of life.

The mere fact that you are reading this book means that you are at least interested in improving yourself. That is leadership. This chapter is intended to help you become a better leader. You will never become a perfect leader. The study of leadership is a lifelong pursuit. If you want to become a great leader, you must constantly practice your craft and never stop studying.

Great Leaders Are Made Not Born

If you are saying to yourself, "I'm not a natural leader," listen up. While there is certainly a portion of leadership ability that comes naturally (think of charismatic leaders such as Bill Clinton), much of it can be learned, studied, and practiced. Charisma can also be developed. You will find that, like other areas of life, you will become a lot more natural at leading others once you actually start leading. There will, of course, be the awkward early stages, but you will eventually become comfortable, and it will start to happen naturally. The overriding theme of this book is to get moving - start taking action - instead of passively watching life pass you by.

Extroverts and Introverts Alike Can Make Great Leaders

We know extroverts when we see them. They thrive on social interaction. It doesn't wear them out - it gives them energy. They are often described as "the life of the party." It is very rare that they don't make themselves known in any given setting. Extroverts have tremendous advantages. They will easily be able to assimilate into their lives the principles outlined in this chapter – and make those principles work to their advantage so they can dominate the second halves of their lives.

We don't tend to notice introverts because they don't demand our attention. Introverts thrive and recharge their energy through alone time. Social settings tend to create feelings of uneasiness within them. This does not mean that introverts cannot succeed and/or become great leaders. In fact, you may not realize it, but history is replete with great introvert leaders. Abraham Lincoln was one of the greatest leaders in our country's history. He was also an introvert. Bill Gates, another introvert, created and led a multi-billion dollar corporation and became one of the richest men in the world. Rosa Parks, recognized as a civil rights leader, and famous for refusing to give up her seat to a white man in 1955, was an introvert and titled her 2000 autobiography "Quiet Strength." Eleanor Roosevelt was a great humanitarian leader and an introvert. She is often quoted as saying "Friendship with oneself is all important, because without it one cannot be friends with anyone else in the world." Mahatma Gandhi, the preeminent leader of Indian nationalism in British-ruled India, and a man who moved millions, was an introvert. He once remarked, "In a gentle way, you can shake the world." These are just a few examples of introverts who became great leaders and made positive contributions to the world. There are many other introverts who have risen to the level of CEO or become successful public speakers.

Basically, introverts can do anything extroverts can do. They just have to break out of their comfort zones a little. They may have to work a little harder at getting comfortable with commanding the attention of others. They have to remember to recharge their introvert batteries by periodically spending some quiet time alone.

What is Leadership?

Leadership is not an easy term or concept to define. We know it when we see it. U.S. Presidents, CEOs, and head coaches are typically good leaders. Of course, there are exceptions to that rule.

We know what leadership is not. It is not the same thing as management. We all know managers who are not good leaders. Leadership is also not dependent on a title or supervisory authority. One co-worker may be a leader among other co-workers. One friend may be a leader among friends. One family member may be a leader of the others, and so on.

At its essence, leadership is the ability to attract people who *want* to follow you, not because of your title or position, but because they truly want to. Perhaps the best way to define leadership is to take a look at some characteristics of leaders that we know to be true. The remainder of this chapter is devoted to examining ten key characteristics that leaders possess -- characteristics you can study and develop in yourself. You may be surprised that several of these characteristics involve acts of giving, rather than taking. In fact, such principles may at first seem counterintuitive. If you really study and think about these principles, however, you will realize that they will make you a stronger leader. You may also be thinking about horror stories you have heard, or experienced firsthand, involving bosses who stole all the credit for their subordinates' work, who used and abused others, and who rose to the top by less than ethical means. Keep in mind that a boss is not necessarily a leader, and that improper tactics are short-term strategies employed by weak individuals. The principles set forth below are for strong ethical people.

1. Listen

Imagine having a conversation with a friend about a problem they are experiencing. Do you cut them off mid-sentence and say something like "I know exactly what you are going through! The same thing happened to me. Here is what I did . . ."? Is that what a leader would do? No. True leaders know that listening is more important than talking. They take the time to listen to everything, to gather all the facts, and to evaluate all possible scenarios before responding. In this way, they help ensure that their response is an appropriate one.

Listening is one of those skills we quickly acknowledge is important, but yet is very difficult to master. It is human nature to be self-centered. We like nothing more than to talk about ourselves. So, becoming a good listener may take a lot of practice.

There are different levels of listening. You can passively listen to someone. Or you can actively listen to them, absorbing all the details and asking appropriate follow-up questions. In order to truly master the art of listening, however, you must develop your empathetic listening skills. This type of listening occurs when you go beyond merely paying attention and asking follow-up questions. You seek to truly understand the other person and the issue they are describing. By developing this skill, you will gain the other person's trust, and you will become a better leader.

You can practice your empathetic listening anytime. You can practice with your spouse, your friends, or at a social event. When you do this, forget about your own needs for a few minutes. Try *really* listening to the other person, seeking to understand them, their needs, and the points they are trying to convey. At the very least, this will make you a more likeable person. In time, it will help you develop one of the characteristics of a great leader.

2. Be Reliable and Trustworthy

In the absence of force, would you follow someone you do not trust? Of course not. Leaders establish trust with others. At its core, this is quite easy. If you have been practicing the Golden Rule since you were a child, you are probably in good shape. If you want people to trust you, then you tell the truth and you do what you say you are going to do. You honor your commitments. You do not make false promises. We all know people who continually tell us they are going to do something, or they make big promises, only to back out or let us down on a consistent basis. We eventually get to the point where we simply don't believe them when they tell us they are going to do something. Think of another type of person who sometimes tells you "yes" and sometimes tells you "no." While you are disappointed when they give you a negative response, you know that when they say "yes" to something, they mean it. They are going to follow through. That person develops a strong reputation with you and you subconsciously trust them a little more. Part of developing this kind of positive reputation is not being afraid to say "no" in the first place. That's infinitely better than becoming known as a person whom others don't take seriously.

We also gain trust with others by treating everyone with respect. There may be people we like more than others. That's human nature. But we can recognize that, at our core, we are all the same. We are all just human beings trying to make it through life. If you treat your fellow human beings with respect – even the ones who get under your skin – you are going to develop a reputation of trustworthiness.

An important aspect of treating others with respect is to refrain from gossip. It is certainly interesting to talk about others and what they may or may not be doing. Leaders do not engage in this practice. Think about the last time you engaged in gossip, either as an active participant or a passive listener. If the person with whom you are speaking is gossiping about someone else, what makes you think they are not also gossiping about you when you are not around? Gossip undermines the trust of everyone involved.

3. Give Freely

If you want to become a respected leader, you must give of yourself before you ever take. In the short term, it is fairly easy for people in leadership positions to take from others. Taking by force or authority of position may work temporarily, but you will never become a strong leader unless you make people *want* to give to you. Begin down this road by giving of yourself. Repeatedly. Never question when it will be repaid. It doesn't matter. If you are always keeping score in life, you are going to be sorely disappointed. After finishing this book, you won't be the type of person who keeps score anyway. You will be a strong person, you will have confidence, and you will be a leader. In any event, if you give freely of yourself, you will most assuredly be repaid many times over in the future. People will remember you. They will also remember those who appear to have ulterior motives. By giving freely of yourself, you will also engender loyalty and respect from others that money or a fancy title could never replicate.

How do leaders give? First of all, they serve others. It sounds counterintuitive. Why would a leader serve others? Aren't servants weak? Quite the contrary. Service to others is actually a hallmark of great strength. In fact, a leader's job is to serve. A CEO serves not only the shareholders, but each and every employee of the company. The President of the United States serves all of the country's citizens. Serving others shows that you are dedicated to achieving the task at hand and that you don't let your ego get in the way of the greater good. So, if you want to become a great leader, start developing a servant's attitude. How can you make others' lives easier? How can you serve your subordinate employees at work? How willing do you think others will be to follow you in the future after you have shown that you will serve them without question? The answer should be obvious.

Next, leaders sacrifice. When someone has to give something, leaders are quick to volunteer. Again, this conveys to their team that they are 100 percent committed to the task at hand. Leaders also work tirelessly to improve the communities in which they live, performing work for volunteer organizations and serving on boards. Leaders are the ultimate team players. While we think of leaders as those at the top who delegate everything (and delegation is an important skill), a true leader is not afraid to get their hands dirty and will chip in wherever and whenever necessary, performing any task, to get the job done. A leader's team members must know that the leader would not ask them to do anything that they would not do.

You will note in the chapter on relationships that giving freely is highlighted there as well. This trait will benefit all aspects of your life, including helping you feel good. So give freely and watch your life improve immensely.

4. Be Decisive

Leaders understand that indecision is a direct path to failure. This is true of life in general. One of the leading causes of an unfulfilling life is that people procrastinate, let indecision rule over them, and neglect to take any action. Do leaders always make the right decisions? Of course not, or else no CEO would ever be fired and every U.S. President would serve two terms. Leaders make decisions, including tough decisions. They take the necessary time to gather all of the important information, they make the decision, and then they don't look back. Decisiveness is not just a characteristic of leaders, but of most successful people. Such individuals have a tendency to make quick, but well-reasoned, decisions, and have the corresponding tendency to not change their minds once decisions are made. Sure, adjustments may be needed, but the overall plan seldom changes once placed into motion. If you want to improve your leadership skills, work on becoming more decisive.

5. Be Influential

You do not need a fancy title to lead others. You do need to be able to influence them. Leaders influence those around them, including family, friends, and co-workers. Leaders are those to whom others turn for guidance because they trust and value what they have to say. How do you become an influencer of others? By being knowledgeable and credible. By sharing your knowledge. By showing genuine interest. By practicing empathetic listening. By giving honest feedback. By giving of yourself. By mentoring younger and less experienced colleagues. By not judging others and not engaging in gossip about them.

A subordinate employee can even lead a supervisory employee once they have become established as indispensable. How do you become indispensable? Well, there are a number of ways: volunteering for difficult assignments, looking for novel solutions to problems, or lending a hand when others are in dire straits. Most assuredly, these are not always the most pleasant situations, but they are the ones that set you apart.

By systematically doing these things, you will slowly but surely become indispensable. You may not have a fancy title, but your boss will come to respect and value your advice. They will not want to make a move without consulting you. You have become a leader and wield considerable influence.

6. Empower Others

This will be one of the more difficult leadership principles for most people to master because it almost seems counterintuitive. Leaders do not hoard power. They do not hog all of the credit for successes. They give power and credit to others. They delegate as much as possible. They take the time to mentor the next generation and to create additional leaders. These actions make them stronger, not weaker. Hoarding power and credit may work in the short-term, but it never does in the long run. This book is all about the long run.

Some may be fearful of giving away power to subordinates, mentoring them, and making them stronger. If a leader trains their followers well, such that the followers become leaders, then there is no more need for the leader, right? Moreover, the followers who themselves become leaders may jump ship to other companies, leaving the leader without strong employees.

While it may feel counterintuitive, the opposite is actually true. A leader who properly develops their subordinates becomes an even stronger leader in two key respects. First, they become a more well-respected leader to those whom they train. Imagine the "willingness to follow" that is created in those subordinates whom the leader empowers. Who is the stronger leader - the one with followers, or the one with followers who are themselves leaders? The answer is clear.

Second, a company or employer will not overlook for long a leader who develops others into leaders. This is the most valuable contribution an employee can make to an organization. While an employer may not see and appreciate everything the leader does, it will be forced to recognize that the leader is responsible for churning out other leaders, for making the organization greater as a whole, and, consequently, creating a more profitable organization.

In addition to empowering others, leaders give credit where credit is due. True leaders do not take all of the credit because they don't need it in the first place. They are self-confident and would rather see their followers receive some well-deserved kudos. A true leader relishes seeing their followers becoming stronger. Of course, the stronger the followers, the stronger the leader.

7. Take Calculated Risks

Leaders understand that playing it safe will enable others to quickly pass them by. There are many examples throughout history of enterprises that were initially very successful, then started playing it safe, only to be surpassed by competitors who were willing to take some risks. General Motors played it safe and saw its market share eroded by companies willing to introduce more innovative products. Sears played it safe and saw competitors like Wal-Mart pass it by and never look back. Playing it safe can often be costly in sports as well. Coaches and their teams often experience a loss when they "play not to lose," while their hungrier opponents "play to win" by taking more risks. Too many people are walking through life playing not to lose. They are so afraid of losing that they won't take any risks. Great leaders know that they are never going to win unless they are willing to take some risks. Not haphazard risks, but calculated risks. Leaders gather the information they need before making decisions, including risky decisions.

8. Set the Right Priorities

Action is important. Indeed, it is the overriding theme of this book. Leaders understand, however, that action by itself does not necessarily accomplish anything. Nor does efficiency. If you establish a highly efficient team, but they are working towards the wrong goal, then you haven't really accomplished anything. Leaders know that they must take action on the right things at the right time. Otherwise, they are wasting time. So, how do you know what the right things are? Well, certainly, you will develop a leadership intuition the more you develop your leadership skills. If you are not yet to that point, then you gather the relevant information, use your reasoning skills, and decide upon the correct actions. You prioritize these actions in basically the same way you do when you are practicing good time management, making sure the biggest most important tasks get taken care of first.

9. Choose Great Advisors

Leaders recognize that no one ever achieves their greatest success alone. Having a trusted group of close advisors is key. Your advisors should be people with whom you regularly interact and whom you completely trust. They can offer you feedback on projects and give you perspectives on ideas you may have for charting your business. In turn, you may provide the same things to them. This is typically, but not always, a two-way street. You may have a mentor-protégé relationship with one of your advisors, where you typically only receive advice.

Your group of advisors is not necessarily the same as your group of friends, although there may certainly be some overlap. Good friends don't necessarily make good advisors and good advisors don't necessarily make good friends. Your advisors should include some people from the same line of business as you. After all, they share common experiences and know your particular industry well. Your group should also contain individuals in different lines of work. These people will be able to give you an external perspective and shed new light on issues with which you may be dealing.

How big of a group of advisors should you have? That depends on you and your circumstances. Certainly you will want at least two to three members. In most cases, a really large group will be unwieldy and ultimately unproductive. So, somewhere in the range of five to six people will probably be comfortable for most people.

Where do you find your advisors? The best groups come together naturally, although there is nothing wrong with seeking out certain people. Your group will probably consist of at least one of your co-workers. This tends to happen naturally. Through networking, you will also meet and develop relationships with people outside of your workplace. When speaking with these people, you will likely come across those with whom you both have a realization that you have chemistry, are ambitious, and are on an upward-bound path to greater success and achievement. So, you will naturally fall into each other's groups.

You may have to make adjustments to your group of advisors from time to time as your life and career develop. This is a natural part of your evolution as a leader. As you develop and grow stronger, you will naturally surround yourself with stronger group members. You have probably heard the advice before. Take a look at your group. If you are the smartest one in it, you need a new group! You may have also heard it said that you are the product of those with whom you spend the most time. So, think about who those people are in your life. You are likely to be the average of those people in terms of success, income, and even attitudes about life. There is nothing selfish or wrong about evolving your group of advisors. The best thing you can do for your family and friends is to be the best version of yourself and inspire them to do the same. If others want to stick with you, then they will have to develop as well.

10. Just Lead

When in doubt, leaders lead. When all else fails, leaders lead. When no one else wants to do it, leaders lead. Leaders don't just talk. They take action. They demonstrate leadership through their actions. Ask yourself what is more convincing: a leader who gives an order and sits back to watch their subordinates carry it out - or a leader who gives an order and then joins in the effort. While it may not be practicable for a leader to join in every activity, their subordinates should know from experience that the leader will not give an order to do something that they would not also do. The leader should be out front, leading. The leader is the ultimate team player in an organization. While they may have the position of authority, they are not afraid to get their hands dirty and work on any task that needs completed.

Leaders persist even after they experience failure. Famed leadership author, John Maxwell, has written several books about failure, including *Failing Forward* and *Sometimes You Win – Sometimes You Learn: Life's Greatest Lessons Are Gained From Our Losses*. Why does a leadership expert write so much about failure? Because understanding that failure is an inevitable part of life, and learning from it, is a great characteristic of a leader. Unsuccessful people let failure defeat them. Successful people, including great leaders, learn from their failures and use them to achieve even greater success.

Finally, leaders determine where their team is going next. They gather the relevant information and then chart the course. Meanwhile, they are always on the lookout for opportunities. As with time consciousness and money consciousness, leaders develop a leadership consciousness. They continuously ask themselves if any particular moment is a leadership opportunity. This comes with experience. The more you lead, the more leadership conscious you will become.

Questions to Ponder

1. In what areas of life do you currently serve as a leader?

2. How can you become a leader without the benefit of a particular title?

3. What one small step can you take today to enhance your leadership ability?

4. How well do you truly listen to others?

5. How well do you believe others trust you, and what can you do to enhance your reputation in that regard?

6. When was the last time you gave all of the credit to others, and kept none for yourself?

7. Who are the people with whom you spend the most time? Do they all have a positive impact on you? Are there changes you need to make to this group?

7 BUILD BETTER RELATIONSHIPS

If you want to go fast, go alone. If you want to go far, go with others.

- African proverb

Relationships Are Crucial

Relationships are everything when it comes to both personal and professional fulfillment. At the end of your life, none of the material possessions you have acquired will matter. Your greatest treasure will be the relationships you have forged over the years.

When it comes to success, your relationships really help determine how far you will go. Knowledge alone is unlikely to enable you to reach all of your goals. Relationships alone may get you a little further. The reality is, to be the best you can possibly be in life, you need both. It is important to have good relationships in your personal life too. The better the network you have, the easier it will be to overcome many of life's obstacles.

While the term "networking" will be used from time to time in this chapter, networking is not the goal. Positive relationships are the goal. Networking is simply an act we perform every day in our professional and personal relationships, whether we realize or like it. It should never be our goal.

This chapter will speak primarily in terms of professional relationships, but because this is a book about getting back on track professionally *and* personally, personal relationships will be discussed as well. In any event, keep in mind that most of the ideas presented will help you in developing *both* types of relationships.

Why Build Relationships?

As a human being, you should want to build relationships for the fulfillment they bring to you - and the fulfillment you can provide to others. We only get one chance at life. Certainly you would rather spend that one life building positive healthy relationships, as opposed to only looking out for yourself at the expense of others.

In any event, whatever your motivation, good relationships are certainly worth their weight in gold. Professionally, relationship-building will help you grow your business, retain clients, and climb the corporate ladder (if that is what you have set out to do). Personally, relationship-building will help create a strong network of friends. You and your friends provide each other with companionship, laughter, and support when needed.

Relationship-Building 101

Establishing positive relationships takes time, effort, and persistence. When and where does relationship-building occur? Everywhere and all the time. If you stop and think about it, you are constantly taking actions that affect every relationship you have or hope to have. When you stop to greet the janitor as you enter your workplace, you are building a relationship. When you go to lunch with your co-workers, you are building relationships. Certainly, we all appreciate that, when we go to business dinners, we are building relationships. While the goal is to always be "building" good relationships, our actions may not always have a positive impact. Our interactions with others can and sometimes do have negative effects. Think of all of your recent interactions with others. Do you treat everyone with equal respect, or do you treat some people better, depending upon whether they have power or the ability to assist you in some way?

After coming to the realization that we are always impacting relationships, either positively or negatively, we must eliminate any "what's in it for me?" mentality we may have. If you have been to enough "networking" events, you can sense this attitude from a mile away. Those people who work the room like an infomercial salesperson, constantly hand out business cards, and immediately ask for your business come off as phony. No one wants to converse with these people, let alone build relationships with them.

If you want to effectively build relationships with others, you must give, give, and give some more, before you ever expect to receive. This may sound like a lot of work. It is - if you treat it like work. You will never be good at relationship-building if you do not learn to love the process. Just like one has to love the process of writing to be able to complete an entire book, one can only successfully build relationships if they enjoy the process of building them. Give because it feels good and is the right thing to do. You will learn to forget about the expectation of "what's in it for me?" and focus on the needs of others. Slowly but surely, a vast network of people will begin to appreciate you for these traits. Then, you will never need to ask for business or help - it will flow to you naturally because people will *want* to help you.

Take a moment to reflect upon the realizations that (1) your actions are always impacting your relationships with others and (2) you should always be giving and never be thinking about receiving. If you ultimately accept these two statements as true, how will that acceptance impact your interactions with others going forward?

Internal Relationship-Building

We often overlook the opportunity to build positive relationships within our own workplace. When we think of networking, we think of developing relationships with individuals external to our organization. As with a lot of things in life, however, we would be well-served in returning to the basics. We should be networking and developing positive relationships with our work colleagues on a daily basis. One of the few certainties in life is that change is constant. Your co-workers will not always be your co-workers. They may move on to other organizations, start their own businesses, become clients of your organization, obtain political office, or make any number of other career moves. If you have made a positive impact on them, and developed good relationships, these people will become part of your external network. So, never overlook the opportunity to network with people internal to your organization (and that means *everyone*, not just those who you perceive as having some current level of power).

Planning to Network

Most successful people have written goals and plans. As it relates to networking, you can assure yourself a greater chance at success by coming up with a written plan. So, get out a pen and paper, or your favorite electronic device, and jot down some notes. Yes, again. You will never make yourself accountable if you do not write down your plan. Moreover, the act of writing things down forces you to be completely honest with yourself. It may also make you realize things you never considered before. Don't worry about what you write - you are the only one who ever needs to see it.

Know What You Do

Start by writing a description of what you do. Sounds easy, right? Unfortunately, however, many people have trouble articulating exactly what they do for a living. If other people don't know, or don't understand, what you do, how could they ever help you? Have you ever asked someone what they do for a living, listened to their response, and then walked away having no idea what they actually do? It happens all the time because people don't put any forethought into their response. You will be in a much better position to verbally articulate what you do for a living if you spend some time alone putting it in writing. Write down a description of what you believe your personal "brand" to be. What are your skills? How do your skills relate to your profession? Are you the "go-to" person in a certain area? Taking the time to write out all of these items will give you a better appreciation for what you have to offer.

After you have written down a full explanation of what you do, take that and pare it down into something you can verbally communicate to someone in both 15 and 30 second sound bites (i.e., your "elevator pitch"). These versions should obviously include the most interesting aspect of your job as well as your value-adding proposition. You will know which version to use by the situation you are in and how much time you have.

Become an Expert

Developing an elevator pitch is the easy part. The real work comes in being able to back up what you say. There is no shortcut in this department. You need to be ready to answer questions and demonstrate your expertise. You need specific knowledge about your field, products, current news, and the competition. People will expect you to be able to converse intelligently about these subjects. This likely means you need to devote extra time outside of work to learning. Your knowledge may come from talking to others, reading trade journals, or having online discussions. The quickest way to become an expert on a given subject, however, is to write or speak about it. This forces you to quickly but thoroughly learn about a topic, and be able to explain it to others. You will not only have a publication and/or speaking engagement to list on your bio, but you will be able to share your knowledge with others during networking events. Speaking and writing also have the added benefit of gaining publicity for you. So, if you can take advantage of these methods, you definitely should.

Know Your Market

Write out a description of your target market by answering these questions: (1) what is my product or service?; (2) who buys my product or service?; and (3) why do they buy it? Next, make a list of your current connections by jotting down a list of who you already know and how they can help you, including family, friends, co-workers, former classmates, etc. Finally, write out a list of connections that you would like to make and jot down some bullet points as to how you can make these connections.

Networking With a Purpose

There is nothing inappropriate about networking with a purpose. In fact, you should be doing this most of the time. Otherwise, you are wasting the opportunities presented by networking events. Certainly, there are occasions when you just want to attend an event and casually enjoy socializing, and that is fine. Most of the time, however, you will want to plan your networking strategy. For example, you may need to generate some new business leads, or begin trying to find a contact who can help you obtain a new position. Thus, you will want to do some advance planning. While it would be easy to criticize this approach as disingenuous, it is just as easy to describe it as the opposite. What could be more genuine that someone who is enthusiastic to meet you and thinks you can help add value to their lives?

Just as you can generate an overall written plan for your networking strategy, you can develop a written plan for specific events. Again, there is nothing wrong with researching the attendees of a social event and targeting certain people you would like to meet. In fact, you should definitely be emphasizing quality over quantity anyway. You may be able to obtain information about attendees online, by request to the event organizer, or from another attendee.

The Art of Networking

You have done your advance planning. You are on your way to becoming an expert in your field. You know yourself and your market. Now comes the fun part. You are at a networking event. What do you do? You have fun, be yourself, and enjoy the moment. You will meet some interesting people, some boring people, and possibly some rude people. That fact alone is fascinating. Think of all the different types of people you will meet. Don't be concerned with the ones who are boring, obnoxious, or rude. Just like everyday life, you have to sort through these people to get to the real gems. So, just take it in stride. Besides, they will probably provide you with some interesting stories along the way.

If you walk into a social event and feel awkward, you are not alone. Most people feel that way entering into any new situation – it is a perfectly natural feeling. Networking is like exercise. You are going to feel awkward the first few times you do it. If you can force yourself through those first few times, it will begin to feel much more natural to you.

There are a few general tips that will help you in any networking event. First, be yourself. Don't be "plain vanilla" and don't be afraid to show your real personality. Authenticity matters and enthusiasm is vital to your success. Just as you should not be fake when building a romantic relationship, you should likewise be genuine when building professional relationships. Many people are afraid to show their true personalities when that is actually the best thing they could do. We get so worried about offending people, or being perceived as weird, that we tend to not reveal any of the more interesting aspects of our lives. Don't be afraid to talk about your hobbies or interesting books you've read. You never know where you are going to find common ground with someone, and that is exactly what will yield the most benefits. Maybe you have a passion for running marathons, but you think no one else would be interested in that. Mention it. Some may find it interesting. Some will reveal they have the same passion. Some may find it weird and move on to someone else. Don't worry about them. Worry about the ones with whom you connect. You are only going to find such connections by revealing your true self. If you present a plain vanilla person, you are not going to stand out, and you are unlikely to make any genuine connections.

While sharing interesting facts about yourself is great, your first priority should be learning about others. Try to find common ground with your audience. You can generally tell if a particular topic is of interest to someone by their nonverbal expression and the level of excitement they show. If they are not interested, move on to a new topic quick! Pay attention to others, listen to them, and listen with the goal of understanding them.

Don't forget the basics, such as a firm handshake and making eye contact. Finally, learn to use people's names. There is no sound more pleasing to the ear than that of one's own name. If you struggle with remembering people's names, it is probably because you are nervous and thinking too much about what you are going to say next or what others are thinking of you. As you attend more and more social events, you will learn to relax and it will be easier to remember people's names. In the meantime, here are some general tips that may help. First, as soon as someone introduces himself or herself to you, try to use their name shortly thereafter. For example, "and where are you from, Lucy?" Try to use their name two more times - once more in conversation and then again as you conclude the conversation: "it was nice meeting you this evening, Lucy." It would also be beneficial to end the conversation by noting something personal that you learned about Lucy. For example, "It was nice meeting you this evening, Lucy. Best of luck with your speech next week." This will not only help you remember Lucy, it will create a positive impression in her mind - you have demonstrated that you were listening and took a genuine interest in her.

Listening

People absolutely, beyond a shadow of a doubt, enjoy talking about themselves. If you are an expert on a subject, it is easy to talk about it, right? And isn't everyone an expert on themselves? You can take advantage of this fact to become the best networker in town. Simply by listening.

Listening is one of the most valuable skills you can master. If you establish yourself as a good listener, people will adore you. The friends, business, and followers will come. People will look to you as a leader and trusted advisor. Listening sounds so easy, but it is not. You must go beyond mere passive listening. Strive for active listening and, ultimately "empathetic listening," where you truly seek to understand and appreciate what the other person is saying.

You can practice your listening skills anytime and anywhere. You can practice at your next social event, with your friends, or with your family members (which may prove to be the most challenging). Truly listen to them. Don't interrupt. Don't turn the conversation back to you. Ask them thought-provoking follow-up questions, such as "how did that make you feel?" When appropriate, briefly summarize what they have said to let them know you are attempting to understand them completely. For example, "so, you were concerned your son wasn't progressing like he should, and that's why you switched programs? That makes sense."

While you are practicing your listening skills, you can play a fun little game with yourself. This game will help you realize what a great job you are doing at networking - and how poorly others may be doing. As you meet new people at a social event and practice your empathetic listening with them, see how many people turn the conversation back towards you and how many are content to talk about themselves 100 percent of the time. The numbers may surprise you. They will certainly make you feel a little better about your skills. And you can take satisfaction in knowing the fact the conversation did not turn towards you has probably created positive thoughts about you in the other person's mind. They think you are great!

Take a Wingman

Networking with a new crowd can feel awkward and uncomfortable. Like everything in life, the more often you do it, the easier it will become. There will even come a point when walking into a room of strangers alone sounds exciting to you. Until you reach that point however, consider taking a "wingman" with you - a friend or colleague who can serve as your "home base" during the networking event. Whenever one of you finds themselves standing in the middle of a crowded event all alone, they can always check in with the other for a few minutes. You can introduce each other to the people you meet and you will never feel isolated. It works great so give it a try.

Tactfully Ending a Conversation

We've all experienced networking events where we end up talking to one person most of the time, either by choice, or because we feel trapped in the conversation. Of course the purpose of networking is to circulate and mingle. Those who have mastered the art of tactfully ending conversations don't get stuck talking to one person. Most of us are familiar with the typical methods of getting away when we feel stuck: "well, I'm going to go get a drink," or "I need to go make a call," or "I think I see my wife motioning for me over there." The problem with these methods is that they involve a little dishonesty. As we learned as children, honesty really is the best policy. Just say something like, "hey, it was great meeting you, I'm going to circulate a bit and try to meet a few more people. Good luck with your speech next week, Lucy." There is nothing offensive about ending the conversation that way and it will probably remind the other person that they should be doing the same thing. Plus they will subconsciously love the fact that you remembered their name.

Relationship-Building Meals

Meals are an excellent way to help build and maintain relationships. They provide a relaxed atmosphere, outside the formalities of work or networking events, that allows you get to know others better. Everyone has to eat and there are 21 opportunities every week to share a meal with someone. People will rarely turn down a free meal. If you have not made networking meals a part of your life, then challenge yourself to begin by scheduling one networking meal per month. You can start with people you already know (particularly those you haven't seen in awhile), but work your way up to scheduling lunches with new people that you can get to know better. You'll be glad you did.

Relationship-Building Through Service

As with leadership, service activities are a great way to expand your relationships. They are especially good for meeting people outside of your particular industry and people you may not otherwise get to meet. Of course, the primary benefit of service is that you get the chance to help others and your community, feeling good about yourself in the process. There are any number of ways to serve your community. You can volunteer for local service organizations, your church, or community outreach projects. You can serve on a nonprofit board, or you can organize your own service projects. The only limitation is your imagination. A great way to build camaraderie among your colleagues is to participate in a service project together. If you work in a white collar profession, a project where you and your colleagues can get your hands dirty will be especially beneficial as you get to interact outside of the normal context. You will learn things about each other that might otherwise never have been mentioned. Finally, as you consider various service projects, think about whether there are particular projects or organizations that mesh well with your career specialty. If you can make such a match, the dividends for you and the project/organization will be tremendous.

Social Media

Social media is a great way to get and stay connected with others. If you are one of the few remaining people who are still resistant to engaging in this form of communication, you should reconsider. The most-cited reason I typically hear is "I like to keep my life private." Well, it is not as private as you think. Anyone motivated enough could pretty easily figure out your daily routine, those with whom you spend time, and so on. Moreover, social media is not nearly as scary as you think. Just treat your social media communications the same as you treat your real world communications. That is, don't do or say anything on social media that you wouldn't do or say in real life.

On the flip side, don't let social media become your only method of connecting with others. We have seen the millennials and younger generations, who are so adept at using technology, lose a step or two when it comes to actual in-person communication. Face-to-face communication is still vital. Make social media one part of your relationship-building arsenal, not the only part.

Social media is a great way to catch up with high school classmates and others you may have lost touch with over the years. It is also a great way to share a little about your personality with others. Just be yourself, which will likely resonate with people much more than being plain vanilla. Some people keep separate personal and professional social media profiles, and that is perfectly fine. Personally, I believe that trying to compartmentalize your life is simply another way of adding stress. Besides, if you are not doing or saying anything on social media that you wouldn't do or say in real life, why does it matter if your "online friends" contain both personal and professional contacts? That's just my opinion. The important thing is that you are using social media to connect with others.

Twitter and LinkedIn are also very popular social networking tools. Sending "tweets" via Twitter, which are 140 characters or less, is a particularly good method of updating your clients and contacts on recent activities, articles you have read or published, and events you will be attending. LinkedIn, of course, basically a professional version of Facebook, and has adapted to include a lot of the same features, such as a "news feed" showing what your contacts are doing. LinkedIn, even more than Facebook, is becoming almost mandatory for professionals. It is a great place to showcase your bio and match yourself and others with those in need of particular expertise.

Maintaining Relationships

As you work to establish a good network of professional connections, keep in mind that this is only the beginning of the process. You must now begin a consistent plan of following up.

Building and maintaining relationships is a process that is never complete. Maintaining relationships is even more important than forming new ones. Complacency can be the death knell to a successful network of relationships. The following steps can help you maintain your professional relationships: (1) Keep your relationships in the loop. Newsletters, blogs, and email lists are easy ways to update your network on news and events that may be important to them. Inviting referral sources to "thank you" lunches is always a nice touch. (2) Help others establish new connections. (3) Keep your knowledge up-to-date. Attend conferences in your discipline (this also presents additional networking opportunities). (4) Keep apprised of developments in your contacts' lives and let them know about it by sending timely congratulatory or other types of notes.

Developing a Group of Advisors

You will not achieve all that you desire in life by working alone. Henry Ford did not act alone. The President does not act alone. CEOs do not act alone. Maintaining a close circle of trusted advisors is absolutely critical to personal and professional success. This inner circle can include as many people as you like but, by definition, it should be somewhat limited. These relationships can be purely professional, personal, or a combination of both.

Developing and Maintaining Personal Relationships

The same general rules that apply to developing professional relationships apply to friendships and other personal relationships. The first rule is always to be yourself. It is tempting to pretend to be someone other than your true self when you first meet someone. You want them to think the best of you. Ultimately, you are hurting both that other person and yourself. You don't want to develop relationships where you have to be fake. These relationships are never going to be enjoyable for anyone in the long run. If you are not enjoying yourself, why bother? The second rule is, once you have started to establish a friendship, give freely of yourself. All relationships require work. It should be work that you *want* to do because you value the relationship. If someone is a friend, especially a close friend, let that person know by the actions you take. Follow the Golden Rule of treating your friends the way you would expect to be treated. In fact, treat them better than you expect to be treated. After all, they are your friends and they bring value to your life just by being there.

As with professional relationships, maintaining your personal relationships is very important. Consider the current state of your personal relationships. Have you contributed to them like you should? What more can you do? In his books on leadership, renowned author and speaker John Maxwell talks about a concept called "relationship capital." Think of all of your relationships like bank accounts. You make contributions to these accounts. You make withdrawals from these accounts. If your withdrawals start to add up without any contributions on your part, then your relationship deteriorates and may ultimately disappear. Sure, you are busy. We are all busy. But your relationships will notice if you have "checked out." Even your most understanding and good-natured friend will eventually feel slighted. We all get busy with a variety of things, but don't forget to periodically check in with your important relationships. It will be worth the effort. After all, wouldn't you want the same done for you? Giving freely is actually the easy part of building good personal relationships. Now comes the tricky part. What about when your spouse, significant other, or friend doesn't behave exactly as you would like? Perhaps they have not done what they said they were going to do. Perhaps they have cancelled on you four times in a row. Perhaps they have told someone something that you shared with them in confidence. Perhaps they are slow to respond to your communications. It doesn't take long to create a whole list of grievances regarding your personal relationships. If you stop and think about these grievances, however, you will find that they have much more to do with you, and your attitudes about how others should act, than they do with the other people. It is exceedingly difficult to change other people. Their egos spring into action, they throw up defense mechanisms, and they will typically point the finger right back at you. So, concentrate on the one person you can control - you.

Acceptance and Forgiveness of Others

Sometimes you do have to let others know how you feel, or tell them your position on a certain subject. That's perfectly healthy. If you want to be happy and feel more at peace, though, the most important skill you can develop is to accept others and to let most, if not all, perceived slights just disappear. Accept the fact that everyone is completely different. We all have different personalities. We all do things a little differently. Embrace these differences in your personal relationships.

Acceptance can be tricky if you are not used to it. Let's go over some methods for implementing it. Keep in mind that most of this advice is not new. Dale Carnegie wrote in *How to Win Friends and Influence People* that you will go a lot further in life, and gain more friends, by being agreeable rather than disagreeable. So, instead of being quick-tempered, be quick to forgive. Our egos prevent us from doing this most of the time. Our egos are offended by the way others, especially friends, treat us. Our egos want to engage and show others that we are right and they are wrong. Try giving your ego some rest and immediately forgive others for perceived slights, even if that means just forgiving them in your head. Are you afraid that this would be a sign of weakness? It is actually a sign of great strength. You don't let things bother you and you don't dwell. You are so strong that you can afford to give more of yourself than you hope to receive in return. Who is stronger – the person who lets others affect them so much that they can't stop thinking about it – or the person who quickly forgives and moves on to more productive aspects of life? The answer is obvious.

Dropping Labels and Expectations

One of the best things you can do to feel better about all of your personal relationships is to drop your labels, expectations, and scores regarding them. Let's start with labels and expectations because they go hand-in-hand. It can be fun and comforting to label others: John is a *good* friend. Lucy is one of my *closest* friends. Mike is my *best* friend. Sally *used to be* my friend until she disrespected me. Doug is the *worst* friend I ever had. The problem with labels is that they are illusory. We have made these up in our minds, without much input from anyone else. We use them because they make us feel comfortable. They allow us to categorize people so that we know what to expect from them. Unfortunately, these labels and expectations just set us up for disappointment after disappointment. Mike was supposed to be my *best* friend, but he has let me down three times in a row! Lucy was one of my closest friends. I can't believe she betrayed my confidence!

The main problem with placing so much expectation on others is that we are simply not those other people. We don't know what they are thinking. We don't know what is going on in their lives. Maybe they are depressed. Maybe they are deeply in debt. Maybe they are having marital problems. You are not them. So, stop expecting them to act like you, or to act any particular way at all. They are never going to act exactly the way you want them to act, so let go of this futile exercise and stop expecting so much from them. Likewise, let's drop the labels that we have placed on everyone. Lets just accept our friends as friends and then forget about it. Then, the next time Lucy betrays your confidence, while you may think twice about what you share with her in the future, she'll still be your friend and you'll immediately forgive her, because you didn't place a label or expectation on her in the first place.

Stop Keeping Score

Has your spouse asked you to watch the kids four times this month and you have only asked once? Have you asked your friend out to a social event three times in a row without receiving a return invitation? If you have given any thought to these types of things, then you are a scorekeeper in your relationships. Stop. Keeping score is a direct path to feeling completely dissatisfied. When we keep score, we are pitting "us" against "them." We are subconsciously creating adversarial relationships with the very people we should be cherishing. We are hurting ourselves in the process. You are never ever going to be happy and content if you keep score with others. You are either going to feel like you owe them or, more likely, they owe you. Keeping score is more a sign of weakness than strength and just another way of placing labels and expectations on others, so let go of it immediately if you want to enjoy better relationships. Sure, you may have to talk to your spouse if you feel they are gone too much, but that's different than saying "you owe me." So what if you have invited your friend to three different events and they have not done the same for you? That person is your friend – your friend whom you acknowledge has a completely different life and personality than you do. Besides, you are strong enough to give freely of yourself without worrying about a return reward. So, don't give it another thought.

Letting Go of Relationships

Now that we have discussed all the positive things we should be doing in our relationships, we come to the point where we acknowledge that some relationships just aren't working for us anymore. If you are doing everything described above and being the best person you can be, you may nevertheless find that there are some less-than-healthy relationships in your life. Think about your current relationships. Perhaps your employer is preventing you from reaching your full potential. Perhaps you are in a troubled romantic relationship that causes harm to all aspects of your life. Perhaps someone who is your "friend" is actually one of your worst enemies. Maybe that person is taking advantage of you or trying to sabotage you. Certainly there are some who will deliberately try to harm you for their own benefit. Hopefully, those people are already few and far between in your life. The more likely scenario is a friend who subconsciously wants you to stay at the same level as them. They may discourage you from taking positive steps forward because they do not want you to leave them behind. Another type of problematic friend is the negative thinker. They rarely see the positive in life. This is counterproductive to your efforts to move forward.

As mentioned earlier, we tend to be the product of the people with whom we spend the most time. If you spend time with people who gripe about how the boss is holding them down, how the world is out to get them, and/or how they will never "make it" in life, then you are very likely to develop similar beliefs and attitudes. If you spend most of your time with people who work just hard enough to get by, then you are likely to engage in that same practice. If you spend most of your time with people of a certain income level, then you are unlikely to move much beyond that level.

Imagine, however, that you spend your time with friends who not only genuinely care about you, but are also "success conscious," meaning that they are constantly thinking about, and working towards, success. These friends are not only concerned with their own success, but with yours as well. They want to lift you up instead of bring you down. These people help you refocus on positive thinking when you have a moment of weakness and let negativity enter your life. Aren't these the people with whom you should be spending your time? You know who these friends are.

They are the friends that make you feel better and give you an energy boost just by their presence. They help you find your smile. Hopefully, you already have at least one such person in your life. If not, don't worry. These people are out there. Be on the lookout for them. If you are working to improve your life, you will, by default, start running in different circles and will meet those people who will remain a positive part of your life.

In the meantime, after some deep thought about your relationships, you realize that there is at least one relationship in your life that is bringing you down in one way or another. It is perfectly okay and natural for relationships to evolve and to end. If you are serious about moving forward in life, it is quite possible that some friends may get left behind. You can try to bring them with you, but the most likely scenario is that not everyone will want to come along for the ride.

If you need to move on from a relationship, you can approach it in one of two ways. Obviously, in an employment or romantic relationship, you will have to formally break things off, presenting your honest reasons for doing so. Friendship situations are more complicated. It generally makes more sense to just transition the friend into one with whom you spend less time. This tends to happen naturally anyway.

After you have ended a relationship, don't dwell on it. Leave the past in the past. Appreciate past relationships for the value they brought to your life and that's it. It is an absolute certainty that, no matter how much time we spend thinking about the past, that is exactly where it will stay. We all know this. We also know that we have an extremely limited amount of time left to live. Life is too short and we have too much left to accomplish. Why waste even a second living in the past?

Questions to Ponder

1. How well do you work to build positive relationships with *everyone*? What can you do to improve in this regard?

2. Can you clearly explain what you do for a living in 15 seconds?

3. How can you improve your listening skills, starting right now?

4. Do you still make an effort to network with others, or have you become lazy in this regard?

5. Who is in your "inner circle" and do you need to make any additions or deletions to this group?

6. What are your three most important relationships? Do you regularly make contributions to those relationships?

7. Do you believe that others regularly mistreat you? Is the real problem your perception of others?

8. Do you have relationships that negatively affect you? What are you doing to change either the nature or existence of those relationships?

9. Are you presently holding any grudges? How would it feel to drop them with no questions asked? Who would that benefit?

10. Do you keep scores in your relationships? How would it feel to stop? Who would that benefit?

8 GET YOUR FINANCIAL HOUSE IN ORDER

Never spend your money before you have it.

- Thomas Jefferson

Money: everyone's favorite subject! Well, at least as it pertains to receiving it. Many of us don't really like discussing the topic in general. Perhaps, like the subject of death, it reminds us of negative things, such as all of the things we are doing wrong. Certainly, we all have different levels of knowledge and experience when it comes to personal finance. Some of us may work in financial fields and be considered experts. Some may know what they should be doing, but ignore it because it is not the fun option. Others may have simply focused on other priorities thus far in life, including their careers and family, and neglected this area. We may have become good at making money, but not given much thought to *keeping* that money. Regardless of how you have treated personal finance to this point in your life, you should at least recognize that the subject is of critical importance. It directly affects how much money we have now and, more importantly, in the future, when we may not have the ability or opportunity to work for more "new" money.

If you've already perfected your finances, congratulations! You are in an elite minority. As for everyone else, this is *our last best chance* to correct some of the mistakes of the past. Keep in mind, I am not a financial planning professional, so nothing in this chapter is expert financial advice. I have friends who are financial experts, and they perform a valuable service. In fact, after reading this chapter, you may decide that you need to consult such a person. As for me, I am a just a regular guy who has studied personal finance in my spare time, because it is in my own best interest. I have no vested interest in trying to sell you on fancy investment techniques or hot stock tips. My only goal is to help you get smarter with your money. The advice in this chapter is time-tested and proven to work. It is the synthesis of hundreds of hours of research and studying. Best of all, it is fairly easy to apply. Unfortunately, for some, this will be the toughest subject in the book. Reasons for that may vary. Certainly personal finance is not the most exciting subject. Moreover, in order to master it, you have to focus on the long-term and work to control short-term impulses. Just like with time management, personal finance forces us to consider our own mortality. We all know that we are going to die someday, but we like to sweep that fact under the rug and never think about it. What should be scarier than the thought of someday dying, however, is the thought of running out of money before we die. The good news is we can stop that from happening. The bad news is we don't have any more "time-outs." So let's do this! I promise it won't take too long or be too painful.

It is often said "its not what you make, its what you keep." We have heard this phrase many times during our lives, but take a moment and really think about it. The statement is absolutely true when it comes to personal finance. What does it matter if you make $250,000 in annual income, but you keep zero at the end of the year? Or worse, you spend more than you make? I am not here to convince you that reducing your expenses and living frugally is the one-way ticket to financial security. Being thrifty may not be enough. You also need to earn to your maximum potential. It is definitely preferable to make $250,000 per year as opposed to $25,000 per year. Thus, you should try to make as much money as you can in endeavors you enjoy. The rest of this book will help you maximize your potential in that regard. This chapter will help you make the most of the financial resources you currently have. It focuses on the fundamentals of personal finance – principles we should all follow, regardless of how much money we make. You can view this chapter as a crash course, guiding you through debt reduction; insurance; saving for emergencies, college, and retirement; and investing basics. Regardless of your experience and knowledge levels, this chapter makes a handy "cheat sheet" regarding the world of personal finance. Even if you know what you *should* be doing, it is often helpful to review written reminders to get you back on track. Just writing this chapter really helped me refocus my financial goals (goodbye sports car, hello additional retirement savings). If you implement the principles in this chapter, earn to your full potential using the advice contained in the rest of the book, then you can cross "money" off your to-do list.

Generation X and Debt

A couple of years ago, my wife and I went out to dinner with another couple. As we paid the check, I noticed that they pulled cash out of an envelope to pay for their share. They explained they had started budgeting a certain amount of money for eating out every month and always paid for things in cash. When the envelope was empty, no more eating out for the month. They had similar envelopes for groceries and entertainment. They tried to avoid any new debt like the plague. I wondered what was wrong with just using credit and debit cards like "normal" people. Even if we spend a little too much, we would keep getting pay increases at work and it would be no problem to pay for it later. Deep down, however, I knew that their way of thinking was infinitely smarter. Most people tend to spend more when using plastic, and it then becomes more difficult to save money for the truly important things in life, like education, a house, or retirement. I always told myself I could self-police my spending and still use my beloved plastic. Besides, all the better for the credit score, right? No. Several years later, I realize that cash truly is king and debt is nothing but a one-way ticket to feeling like a prisoner. I'm not going to tell you that you have to pay cash for *everything*, but I am going to tell you that our generation is way too familiar with debt, and that needs to change right now if we want to make a serious halftime adjustment in the area of personal finance. Are you making the same debt payments now as you were 15 years ago (i.e., house, student loans)? Do you want to be making those same payments when you retire? You may very well be if you don't change your personal finance habits right now.

Unfortunately, Generation X became extremely comfortable with debt, almost from birth. Many of our parents instilled in us that debt was a part of everyday life, not something to be avoided. Many of us watched as our parents lived beyond their means. We watched as the stock market and the economy exploded. We grew up believing we were entitled to go to college. We grew up believing we were entitled to the nice house and car. We grew up believing we were entitled to the American dream, just because we existed. Plus, we had the available tools to aid us in fulfilling our entitlement. We came of age during a time when credit was easy. All of this was, of course, a recipe for disaster when it came to debt. By the time we graduated from college, many of us were already carrying student loan and credit card debt. Why not tack on car and home loans? After all, we were at the beginning of great careers and would be able to easily repay all the money. Plus, real estate values were going to increase every year like clockwork. It was all common sense.

Before we knew it, we found that economic realities had shifted, home values decreased instead of increased, and we were overburdened with debt. Many of us used credit cards to help finance the lifestyles to which we felt entitled. If you ended up in this scenario (it's okay, you can admit it to yourself), you likely increased your debt every month instead of decreasing it. If that is the case, this chapter will help. Like every other chapter in this book, however, the principles outlined here are simple in concept, but will require discipline on your part if they are to prove useful. The magic pill to make your debt disappear has not been invented yet. Bankruptcy you say? Forget what you have heard about any benefits of bankruptcy. It really is a last resort. This is one of those times when the "hard way" is probably easier than the "easy way."

Some Debt is Better Than Others, But Just Barely

You have probably heard people talk about good debt versus bad debt. Some debt is better than others, but there really is no such thing as good debt. You will be exponentially better off if you don't have any debt. It takes money to make money. The higher your net worth (assets minus liabilities), the more money you will be able to make through investments, whether that means interest on your savings, buying stocks and bonds, or starting a business. In any event, there is a pecking order to debt, so let's take a look at some so-called "good" versus "bad" debt. Obviously, we want to eliminate the bad debts as quickly as possible.

Student loan debt ranks as a so-called "good debt," by virtue of the fact that, in exchange for the debt, you have hopefully received an education that will help you earn many multiples of the debt. Education is certainly an investment, so you won't get much argument from me about having student loan debt (it would be too late for such an argument anyway).

Mortgage debt is also typically deemed preferable to other types of debt because the interest is often tax deductible and there is an underlying asset, your house, securing the debt. If you have a $200,000 home with a $100,000 mortgage, you still have a net asset value of $100,000. That doesn't mean you should carry a home loan for the tax advantages. You will still be much better off without any debt at all.

Other types of "secured" debt (for which there is an underlying asset), such as vehicle loans, are next in the pecking order. A

$30,000 car with an accompanying $20,000 loan has a net value of $10,000 on your personal balance sheet. Only rare collector cars will ever have a value higher than the purchase price, and it is almost impossible to tell which cars will end up being collectible. Moreover, we all know that vehicles literally lose thousands in value as soon as we drive them away from the dealership. So, you can see why personal finance experts attack cars and trucks as the source of a lot of bad financial decisions.

Credit card debt is the king of bad debt (well, other than gambling debt). There is no underlying asset backing it up. If you have $10,000 worth of credit card debt, you have $10,000 in debt with no assets to show for it. In addition, this type of debt typically (but not always) carries the highest interest rate. You may be paying 20 percent or more for the purchases you made on your credit cards, including meals, fuel for your car, and gifts for others. It is hard to make forward progress when you are paying out this much interest on the money you have borrowed. Thus, in the next section on paying down debt, you will see that this should typically be the first type of debt you attack.

Paying Down Debt

If you don't have any debt, and some of you don't, which is fantastic, you should do a little victory dance and skip this section. The remaining sections of the chapter will still be important to you. If you do have debt, then you realize what a burden it is on your life. You can easily become a slave to servicing it. You lose the flexibility to make career, investment, or personal financial decisions because your primary focus is making payments on the debt. As in other areas of life, the first step in dealing with debt is admitting you have a problem. If you don't think you have a debt problem, perform the following simple exercise. Write down your *net* (after-tax) monthly income. Then add up all of your fixed debt payments, including mortgage, student loans, car loans, other loans, medical debt, and credit card debt. If your total fixed debt amounts to 40 percent or more of your net income, then you likely find that you run tight at the end of the month. This is because we haven't even figured in all of our variable expenses, which run the gamut from groceries, eating out, and clothes, to more unexpected expenses such as replacing the transmission in the car or buying a new washer and dryer when the old ones give out. Even if your results are less than 40 percent, this is the time of your life where you need to begin the process of making that number as small as possible so that you don't have to worry about debt in retirement.

Paying down debt is a relatively simple process, but it requires a huge commitment and lots of willpower on your part. First, you must at the very least reduce your monthly spending to below your net income. This is critically important. Otherwise, your debt will continue to climb. Too many of our generation have fallen into the trap of living above our means, thinking that our income will increase in the future and we will pay for everything then. While this may happen for the lucky few, reality has shown us that our income will increase incrementally, and we will increase our standard of living in lock-step. Those of us with children know that they get more expensive with each passing year. Thus, we absolutely have to reduce our expenses to somewhere below our net income if we have any hope of ever escaping our debtors' prison. If you are creative enough, you should be able to find many ways to reduce your spending without feeling it too much.

Some ideas are discussed in the next section. If, however, you have reviewed your monthly expenses and just can't find any possible areas to cut, then you need be brutally honest with yourself and consider whether some sacrifices need to be made for your overall financial health. Perhaps a home or automobile downsizing needs to occur. Maybe private school is not absolutely necessary. These are not pleasant decisions by any means, but keep in mind that this may be your last best chance to turn your financial ship around, and that means tough decisions have to be made.

Next, we start paying off our debts. Life is complicated enough, so I like methods of improvement that you can set on autopilot and then forget. With that in mind, after reducing our expenses to below net income, we need to determine how much money we can set aside each month, after all other bills, including minimum payments on credit cards. Say this amount is $500. That is the monthly amount we are going to use to begin to reduce our debt. If you can't get to $500, start with a lower amount. You may also want to go back a step and honestly assess whether there are other ways you can reduce your standard of living. Remember, this is going to be somewhat painful, but well worth it.

Take your $500 (or other amount) per month and apply it towards the highest interest debt first. Once that debt is paid off, take the $500 and apply it to the next highest interest-bearing debt, along with the minimum payment you had already been making on that debt. For example, you had been sending the $500 to Credit Card 1 every month, along with a $100 minimum payment to Credit Card 2. Now, you are sending $600 per month to Credit

Card 2. You are paying your debt off at an even faster rate - and this is the "automatic pilot" part - you don't have to contribute any extra money. Regardless, you repeat this process with all of your remaining debt. Each time, you will be increasing the monthly payment without contributing any new money. Thus, you will be paying your debt off faster and faster. Of course, you should feel free to add additional money (maybe a pay raise) to get even faster results. What order should you pay off your various debts? You may want to pay off your smaller debts first for psychological reasons: you will gain confidence and see that the plan is working. Personally, I like the approach of paying off the higher interest debt first. This will help build your net worth faster. The choice is yours. The important thing is to just get started.

This approach really does work. But it requires persistence. It may take several years. You must live more frugally than you have in the past. If you intensely stick with the plan, however, you will find yourself debt-free exponentially faster than on the plan, or lack thereof, you previously followed. If you don't make a change now, will you ever get out of debt? Isn't your ultimate freedom worth a little sacrifice now? As you proceed with your debt reduction plan, be careful to remain vigilant for the thought in your head that says you deserve something. "Wow, I've paid off half of my debt, I deserve a vacation." Debt elimination must remain your absolute highest priority when it comes to personal finance. As with other concepts in this book, you can eliminate debt with a plan of action, persistence, and a burning desire to make it happen. If you possess these things, you will accomplish your goal.

Making Difficult Choices

Getting smart financially involves cutting out stuff that we know we don't need in the first place, but is fun and comforting to enjoy. The small things really do add up. We fritter away a ton of money every month on things we don't need. If you have read any personal finance literature, you know the five dollar cup of coffee has been repeatedly demonized. I'm not telling you to ditch the coffee. In the whole scheme of things, if that is something you value highly, then you should decide to keep it and eliminate something else. I know I did – coffee is responsible for a large part of this book! But examine your purchasing behavior, think about how you spend your money, and find areas where you can reduce or eliminate. Maybe a small coffee will satisfy you as much as the large one. Maybe you can make the same coffee in your house for a fraction of the price. Ditto with restaurant dining.

While there is no doubt that the small things do add up, there is no substitute for eliminating some of the burden of the big things, like your fixed debt payments. While you are using the debt elimination method described above, you can speed up the process further by getting rid of some of the big items you can easily do without. Can you sell the boat you financed but don't use? Can you trade your luxury car for a more mainstream and economical sedan? Sometimes we have great emotional attachment to these material possessions, but if we really give it some deep thought, we realize that don't actually add much value to our lives.

Becoming Money Conscious

Recall the concept of time consciousness. When you analyze everything in terms of efficient and effective use of time, you start noticing more and more ways you can save time. The same concept applies with money (and other success principles outlined in this book). The more you think about ways you can save money, the more ways it will "magically" appear. This chapter is all about simplicity. We make things too difficult on ourselves. There are smart choices – common sense choices – you can make and then forget about, which will save you money over time. One huge area where you can make a decision and then forget about it is in the area of transportation. This may be a sensitive subject for some. I know it is for me. Some of us absolutely love cars. They are a huge weakness of mine. I have subscriptions to all the major car magazines – a startling admission in a chapter on personal finance! Yes, those subscriptions may be unnecessary spending. They are also a lot cheaper than actually buying a new car whenever the urge strikes. In any event, most people I have encountered are not the same as me when it comes to a weakness for cars. They simply rely on these "appliances" for transportation from A to B. If that is the case, then why in the world would you ever spend more than necessary on these things? Is it because your neighbor or co-worker has a luxury car and you feel the need to keep up with them? Save yourself a lot of trouble and money. Buy a thrifty and reliable car, such as a four cylinder midsize sedan, and then forget about it. Modern cars are, for the most part, all nice with plenty of power and standard convenience features. Most of them look good too, so you won't be embarrassed driving them. They also last longer than you may think. So this is one area where we can truly set it and forget it. Get into the right car (you may already have it) and you'll save money without having to give it another thought. Of course, if you have an extra car that you don't actually need, then it goes without saying that you can find some great financial savings by liberating it from your household.

Other areas where you can make simple decisions that reap long-term financial rewards include adding insulation to your home to save on energy costs and resolving to dine at home more often. In addition, take it easy on your water and electric consumption. We should be doing this anyway, but it is easy to get lazy with these items. I thought my father was crazy when I was a kid. He would always walk around, turn off unnecessary lights, and turn the thermostat down a notch. It seemed to me like that was his hobby. As an adult, I looked around my house a few years ago and there were lights on everywhere. I now walk around turning them off too. I also try to take it easy on water consumption, skipping a car wash here and there. These habits may sound trivial, but adopting them now will save you lots of money automatically over the course of time.

Emergency Savings

Perhaps the most important step on the road to financial freedom is to establish an emergency savings fund. Life is full of unexpected expenses. Your washing machine needs replaced. Your car needs a new transmission. You have an unexpected medical expense. Sure, you can take money out of current income to pay the expense. What if you don't have enough? Then you are forced to pay with credit, beginning the vicious debt cycle discussed above. If you have made it this far in life, you also know that we really should be calling these expenses "expected" rather than "unexpected," because they tend to happen quite often. I used to complain that "something" came up every single month. Now, I just expect and accept it as a fact. I have re-categorized many unexpected expenses as expected expenses for which I can plan. Of course, there are still those truly unexpected expenses in life. Can you make it more than a few months without one? Probably not.

This is where the emergency savings fund enters the picture. This fund's sole purpose is to provide cash for unforeseen expenses. Most people should make an emergency savings fund their number one financial priority, even before paying down debt. While it would be more aggressive to pay down interest-bearing debt first, the establishment of an emergency savings fund is vital in two ways. One, it gets you in the habit of saving. Two, it will help you avoid additional debt in the future. Personally, I decided to start automatically contributing to an emergency savings fund at the same time as aggressively paying down debt. Again, the choice is yours. The important thing is to just take action.

The easiest way to establish an emergency savings fund is to do it automatically by paying yourself first. Determine how much money you can set aside each month for your emergency savings and have it automatically deducted from your paycheck. If you feel like you cannot spare much money, then start your emergency fund with $50 per month. That small amount will turn into $600 (plus interest) in one year. If you can't afford $50, start with $25. Or $15. Just start with something!

Once you have started the emergency fund, make sure it is exclusively a fund for emergencies. You should not use your retirement or college savings as your emergency fund. I have been guilty of this in the past and can recognize now it was just an excuse to get out of doing the right thing. Moreover, your emergency fund should never be mistaken for your "delayed spending" fund. Its purpose is not to help you save for a new television or vacation. You should establish separate savings accounts for those items, if you decide you truly need them. Keep building up your emergency savings until you have enough money to replace three to six months of income. Then you won't have to panic quite as much if you are faced with an unexpected expense or drop in income.

Insurance

We all agree that we need some amount of insurance in our lives, especially if we have families. Some insurance, such as health and auto, may be required by law. What about other, more optional, types of insurance? Even if you are single, you may want to consider disability insurance for use in the event you become incapacitated from working. Certainly it is a rare occurrence, but it does happen. Because incapacity is rare, however, this type of insurance is typically very affordable, depending of course on how much replacement income coverage you need.

If you have a family, then you will definitely want to invest in life insurance to protect your loved ones in the event of an untimely death. The two general types of life insurance are "term" and "whole life." Term insurance is exactly what it sounds like. You have the insurance for as long as you pay the premiums.

There is no real savings component. That is, if you cancel it, you don't have an asset. Nevertheless, term insurance involves lower monthly premiums and is the type most people should select until they get their finances under control. At that point, it may be worthwhile to consider whole life insurance, which involves a higher monthly premium, but acts more as a savings vehicle. You build up a cash value in the policy that may be redeemed for events other than death, depending upon the terms of the particular policy. In other words, a whole life policy is an asset whereas a term life policy is not (unless you die or another qualifying condition is met). If you are interested in whole life insurance, you should consult your financial planner or do independent research to determine whether such insurance is a good choice for you. From a purely investment perspective, whole life insurance may not make the most sense compared to other products offering higher rates of return. Like any investment, however, its attractiveness will depend on your personal situation and risk tolerance.

Saving for Retirement

As a generation, the baby boomers neglected to save enough money for retirement. Generally speaking, they had good jobs making good money, but they became a generation of excess: large houses, luxury cars, vacations, and frequent dining out. Now, in the absence of sufficient retirement savings, many of them face the prospect of working until they die. If you are a boomer and reading this, keep your spirits up because it is never too late to make a big dent in the problem. So keep reading!

Generation X may face a fate similar to the boomers if we fail to immediately address the retirement issue. Moreover, our generation faces additional obstacles that will make a comfortable retirement even more difficult to accomplish. We have come to realize that we cannot depend on social security being there for us. Even if it is, it will not come close to providing us with a quality of life even approaching middle class. The other major change that has affected our generation is that pensions are becoming a thing of the past. Prior generations could work 30-40 years for their employers, and then expect a nice fixed pension during their retirement years. Companies have, for the most part, phased out these plans. Therefore, unless you are guaranteed a large inheritance, retirement is going to be totally up to you.

The first rule of saving for retirement is to begin saving for retirement *right now*, no matter what your age. After establishing plans to build an emergency fund and pay down debt, this is the next most important financial objective for you. If you have not already started, you are well behind in the game. The younger you start saving for retirement, the better, because you will have the benefit of compound interest. A simple example demonstrates the amazing power of compounding. If you were offered the following two options, which one would you select? Option A is $3 million dollars today. Option B is one penny that doubles in value every day for 31 days. Most people would select Option A. That is a lot of money! But, let's take a look at what happens with Option B. On Day One, you have one lonely penny. On Day Five, you have a mere 16 cents. On Day 20, you are up to an impressive $5,243. Just 11 days later, on Day 31, however, you have a whopping $10,737,418. What the heck happened? Over 10 million dollars from a single penny?!? As you can see, the benefits of compounding become even more pronounced during the final stages of a time period. Thus, from this example, as you can imagine, the difference between starting to save for retirement at age 20 versus age 30 is startling. The difference between starting at age 20 and age 40? You don't want to know. The good news is that it is never too late to get started. Whatever your age, you need to start right now.

Thankfully, even though pensions may be a thing of the past, there are many ways to easily and effectively save for retirement. Most employers offer a 401(k) plan, which is a tax-advantaged retirement savings plan you use to save funds for retirement. Traditional 401(k) contributions are tax-deferred, meaning they save you taxes in the current year, but are taxable when withdrawn. If you select "Roth" contributions (offered by some employers), then you pay money on the contributions in the current year, but your withdrawals are tax-free. The choice is yours. Individuals typically choose traditional contributions if they want to minimize the present year's tax bill and/or they believe their income level will be less during their retirement years, which is typical. Individuals select Roth contributions if they believe they will be in a higher tax bracket during their retirement years, or they believe that taxes will rise in the future. Depending on your current versus future anticipated tax bracket, a Roth contribution can yield tremendous tax advantages.

Further adding to the attractiveness of the 401(k), some employers match up to a certain level of contribution. For example, your employer may offer to match the first 5% of income that you contribute. Check with your benefits department to see if your company offers such a match. If they do, and you are not taking advantage of it, you are essentially passing up free money. Unfortunately, like pensions, employer matches have been getting phased out too. So, now more than ever, retirement really is all up to us.

Regardless of whether you get a company match, employer-sponsored 401(k) plans are very convenient savings tools because you can typically set up automatic contributions from your paycheck. This makes saving easy. You don't even have to think about it. Because your contributions are automatically deducted from your pay, you never have the money in your possession, so you don't really miss it.

If you are unable to find money in your current budget to contribute to your retirement, start small with $25 to $50 per month. Cut back a little throughout the month and you should be able to find at least an extra 50 bucks. Then, when you receive a raise at work, place that additional money into your retirement savings as well. You will never miss it because you never got used to spending it. If you repeat this process with each raise you receive, your retirement contributions will eventually be very substantial.

If you are maxing out contributions to your 401(k) plan, and have additional money you want to save for retirement, you might consider opening an Individual Retirement Account (IRA). Contributions to such accounts may or may not be tax-deductible, depending upon your income level and the type of IRA you select. As with 401(k)s, a traditional IRA allows you to take a tax deduction in the current year and a Roth IRA gives you the benefit of tax-free distributions later.

There are other vehicles for saving for retirement, but 401(k)s and IRAs will likely be the primary options for most people. It doesn't make much sense to have a regular investment account until you have maximized your contributions to any tax-advantaged accounts. Any income from a regular investment account is typically taxable and included in your current income each and every year. After you have maximized your tax-advantaged savings, though, an investment account may be a great way to earn some passive income, as discussed in the section on investing below.

Saving for College

If you have children, consider the cost of a college education in present dollars. We are likely talking in excess of $100,000 for tuition, room, and board at an in-state public school. Multiply that by at least two for some out-of-state institutions. Now multiply again by whatever multiple you think appropriate for the number of years your children have until they are ready for college. If you have a toddler now, you may need to budget double the above amounts. It's certainly not going to get less expensive.

There is no rule that says parents have to pay for their children's college education. And some children may decide to get a job or start a business instead of continuing their education after high school. We will assume, however, for purposes of this discussion that our children will continue on to college, and that we will want to provide them with at least some financial support. We can hope for "full-ride" academic or athletic scholarships. That will save us a ton of money! But, of course, those are as rare as winning the lottery. So, we should plan accordingly. As with retirement, your best bet is to make saving for college automatic. That way, you never have the money in your possession, you don't get used to spending it, and you really don't miss it. Sign up for an automatic investment plan and have a certain amount of money withdrawn from your checking account each month, or every two weeks, and placed into a college savings plan.

One popular type of plan is the 529 savings plan, named after section 529 of the Internal Revenue Code. There are two primary tax advantages of these plans. First, depending upon your state of residence, you may be able to take a deduction for current-year contributions to the plan. Second, the earnings on 529 plans grow and are federal tax-free when distributed, so long as they are used for qualified education expenses. If your child decides not to go to college, you can still withdraw the money for other use, but will have to pay tax on it. There will be a variety of investments you can choose from in your 529 plan, just like with your retirement account. As with any investment, there are other important details to consider. Check with your financial institution or advisor to see if a 529 savings plan is right for you.

As with retirement savings, if you feel like you don't have enough current income to save for college, the important thing is to start with something, even if it is $25 per month. That way, you can begin taking advantage of the miracle of compounding. Then, as your income grows, you can increase your level of savings.

Investment Priorities

By now you are probably wondering in what order to prioritize all of these important areas of saving. It can be quite overwhelming for sure. There are several schools of thought. Some would say maximize your retirement savings above all else to take advantage of compounding. Personally, I would place higher priority on paying down debt, both because this typically gives you the greatest bang for your buck, and for the sense of freedom and flexibility it brings. If you are paying 20 percent on debt, but can make 10 percent in the stock market, isn't paying down the debt the better investment – the one that will build your net worth faster? Of course. Then, I would prioritize finishing off an emergency fund, again for two reasons. One, it will help you avoid getting back into debt. Two, it will give you confidence and peace of mind as you proceed further down the road to financial freedom. Next, I would prioritize retirement over college savings. Yes, we all love our children, but there are other ways to pay for college. If you can't retire, you will have to be able to work. If you can't work, you are going to have to depend on your children to support you, which will be a huge financial burden. So, retirement should be your top priority, for the benefit of both you and your children.

Investing Basics

As indicated above, saving for retirement is basically up to you. That means you are going to be faced with some choices regarding how the assets in your retirement account are invested. You may also have one or more non-retirement investment accounts, including college savings accounts. So, you need to know a little about investing. Like everything else in this book, I have tried to take the complicated and break it down into easy-to-understand guidance.

People get paid a lot of money to talk about the stock market. Here is the truth: the stock market goes up and it goes down. No one actually knows what it is going to do on a particular day, week, month, or year. Sometimes the experts get their predictions right. Many times they are wrong. This doesn't mean you shouldn't hire a financial advisor. There are real benefits they can bring to the table, as described below.

Here is another truth: historically, the U.S. stock market has returned about 9.4 percent on our investments. So, that is about what you can expect over the long haul. Of course, over the short term, you can make a lot of money, or lose a lot of money. This chapter is about personal finance, however, not day trading. No matter what you hear from others, day trading is gambling. There are people who have made fortunes in either pursuit. There are many more stories, however, of lives ruined.

Now back to investing. Obviously, 9.4 percent is a lot more than you can currently make on a savings account or certificate of deposit. So, it is easy to see why most people cannot resist the siren song of the stock market.

If you don't have any interest in learning about investing, that's no problem. Life is busy and you should spend your time with the things that interest you. If you are not going to take an active role in investing, you should either hire a financial advisor or at the very least, stick with professionally-managed mutual funds and avoid individual stocks. A financial advisor may not be able to predict the stock market, but they can help you choose investments and set the proper allocation for those investments as you move toward your goals. Hire a financial advisor who works on a fee basis, not a commission basis. That removes the incentive for the advisor to move you in and out of investments, which is generally an unsound strategy given the near impossible nature of timing the market.

If you want to play a somewhat active role in your investing, or cannot afford a financial advisor, then you should study professionally-managed mutual funds. Target-date funds are the easiest. For example, if you are looking at investments for your retirement account, you can select a professionally-managed fund with a target date equal to the year you plan to retire. The fund's manager will determine the proper allocation among investments, such as domestic stock, international stock, bonds, and cash. The allocation will become more conservative (more weighted towards investments like bonds and cash) as the target date nears. College savings accounts, such as 529 plans, typically have target date funds you can choose from as well.

If you have some interest in learning about investing, and don't want to pay others to manage your money, then you can choose some mutual funds and perhaps some individual stocks for yourself. You will also need to determine the appropriate allocation among investments for your age and goals. The allocation is simply how your money is divided among various investments, such as stocks, bonds, real estate, and cash.

Obviously, when you are young and have time on your side, you can set a much more aggressive allocation. By way of example, a 20 year old may want an 80/20, or even a 90/10, allocation between stocks and bonds in their retirement portfolio. Over time, they should shift that allocation so that, by the time they retire, the allocation is basically reversed, or 20/80. There are an infinite number of ways to determine the appropriate allocation for someone. Risk tolerance is a big factor. If you cannot stomach seeing wild fluctuations in your retirement account balance (even with the knowledge that the stock market will return about 9.4 percent over time), then you probably should not set an 80/20 allocation. One method of asset allocation I like is to set your bond percentage to match your age. So, if you are 35 years old, you would set your bond allocation to 35 percent, and so on. You can continue to do this into your retirement years so that you would have a 20/80 allocation by the time you are 80. Keep in mind that, even after you retire, it is probably not necessary to have all of your money in bonds and cash because you are not going to need all of it immediately. The goal is for your money to outlive you, not the other way around.

If you are fairly comfortable with personal finance and investing, then you should seriously consider investing in index funds, as opposed to managed funds. Index funds simply track a sector of the market. For example, there are index funds that track the S&P 500 index (larger companies), the extended market index (smaller companies), bonds, and international stocks. These funds have become more and more popular and there are index funds for just about any segment of the market. What makes them great is that they are *not* actively managed and, thus, their fees are extremely low compared to managed funds. A managed fund with management fees of less than 1 percent is typically considered reasonable. In contrast, however, it is not uncommon for index funds to have management fees of .20 percent or less. In percentage terms, that may not sound like a big deal, but it is basically 1/5 the amount of fees. Compounded over 20 to 30 years, we may be talking about several hundred thousands, or even millions, of dollars, depending upon the amount of money involved. John C. Bogle, founder of the Vanguard Group investment company, is considered by many to be the guru of index funds. If you want to handle your own investments, his book, *The Little Book of Common Sense Investing*, is just about all you need. Personally, I enjoy managing my own selection of index funds. But, that approach may not be for you. If you want to devote as little time as possible to investing, then some degree of professional asset management may be preferable.

Final Bits of Advice

Well, we've reached the end of the road, both in terms of this chapter and this book. Hopefully, you have picked up a few pointers that will help you improve one or more areas of your life. The goal is not perfection – that's impossible. The goal is to become a little better today than you were yesterday. Then repeat. If the first part of your life has gone by in flash, the next part is going to go even faster. You only live once, so get out of your comfort zone, make some halftime adjustments, and chart the course for a successful second half!

Questions to Ponder

1.   Do you avoid the topic of personal finance because you feel you are too young and/or it is just "no fun"?

2.   Do you regularly run out of money before your next paycheck?

3.   Do you feel like a prisoner to your debt? What are you going to do about it?

4.   Do you use debt to finance your lifestyle? When are you going to stop?

5.   Are you prepared to make difficult choices to get your finances in order?

6.   Do you have an emergency savings account?

7.   How are you saving for your retirement and your children's education?

RECOMMENDED READING

There is not much rhyme or reason to this list, other than the fact that these books have been highly influential on me. You cannot go wrong with any of them, although *The Power of Now* and *Think and Grow Rich* have personally influenced me the most, so I would say start with those. Additional recommendations can be found online at www.personfactory.com. These can be life-changing books – if you put their lessons into practice. Enjoy!

The Power of Now by Eckhart Tolle
Think and Grow Rich by Napoleon Hill
As a Man Thinketh by James Allen
My Philosophy for Successful Living by Jim Rohn
The Compound Effect by Darren Hardy
The 1% Solution for Work & Life by Tom Connellan
The Charge by Brendan Burchard
The 7 Habits of Highly Effective People by Stephen R. Covey
How to Win Friends and Influence People by Dale Carnegie
Failing Forward by John C. Maxwell
The 21 Irrefutable Laws of Leadership by John C. Maxwell
The 15 Invaluable Laws of Growth by John C. Maxwell
Be a People Person by John C. Maxwell
Risky is the New Safe by Randy Gage
How to Stop Worrying and Start Living by Dale Carnegie

Never Eat Alone by Keith Ferrazzi
Relationships Are Everything! by Mark Maraia
Falling Into Grace by Adyashanti
The End of Your World by Adyashanti
Sometimes You Win Sometimes You Learn by John C. Maxwell
A New Earth by Eckhart Tolle
Finding Your Element by Ken Robinson
Stillness Speaks by Eckhart Tolle
Stickability by Greg Reid
Practicing the Power of Now by Eckhart Tolle
The Complete 101 Collection by John C. Maxwell
The War of Art by Steven Pressfield

ABOUT THE AUTHOR

Brian J. Moore speaks and writes about various personal development and leadership topics, both for his own good and to help others. He blogs about personal development and leadership at The Person Factory (www.personfactory.com). In addition, he practices labor and employment law in West Virginia and Kentucky. He obtained his business and law degress from West Virginia University and is involved in many civic organizations.

www.ingramcontent.com/pod-product-compliance
Lightning Source LLC
Chambersburg PA
CBHW061146040426

42445CB00013B/1568

* 9 7 8 0 5 7 8 5 3 7 3 8 2 *